R. F. EASTERLY

Bought at Ridgecrest N.C.
July 19, 1952
Visited with Denis Lyle
from Canyon Texas.

NEW TESTAMENT
Life and Literature
as
REFLECTED IN THE PAPYRI

NEW TESTAMENT

Life and Literature

as

REFLECTED IN THE PAPYRI

BY

ELDRED DOUGLAS HEAD

AM., TH.D., D.D., LL.D.

President, Southwestern Baptist Theological Seminary
Fort Worth, Texas

BROADMAN PRESS

NASHVILLE, TENNESSEE

COPYRIGHT, 1952
BROADMAN PRESS
NASHVILLE, TENNESSEE

PRINTED IN THE UNITED STATES OF AMERICA

2.5AT51ABK

Lovingly Inscribed
to

DR. JOSIAH BLAKE TIDWELL

Preacher, Scholar, Christian Statesman

CONTENTS

PREFACE   ix

INTRODUCTION   1

I. HISTORICAL RESUMÉ   8

II. THE NEW TESTAMENT DOCUMENTS   20

III. PHILOLOGICAL REFLECTIONS   35

IV. DOMESTIC RELATIONS   51

V. THE SYSTEM OF TAXATION   68

VI. FISCAL METHODS AND MACHINERY   79

VII. LEGAL TRANSACTIONS   89

VIII. THE TRADES AND PROFESSIONS   101

IX. RELIGIOUS AND MORAL CONDITIONS   114

REFERENCE NOTES   133

ABBREVIATIONS FOR PAPYRUS DOCUMENTS   141

TABLE OF EGYPTIAN MONTHS   142

SOURCE MATERIALS   143

PREFACE

THE MOST alluring field of research offered the Bible student in modern times is that of papyrology. The light reflected from its abundant harvest of documents has effected results beyond the fondest expectation of scholars. The end is not yet, for the future yields may be expected to reveal even richer and more revolutionary facts.

Two leading objectives have been continuously before the author of the following pages: *first,* to provide an adequate background for such a study; *second,* to reconstruct from the papyri the world contemporary with the New Testament. The chapter divisions in the table of contents guide the reader in his study of the two objectives.

The reader's attention is called to some of the features peculiar to the arrangement of the material. Each chapter is introduced with a collection of pertinent Scripture quotations, selected because they make specific reference to the topics elucidated therein. It is believed that such passages will serve not only to reveal the special biblical emphasis on the particular subject under consideration but will also demonstrate the close connection of the New Testament with the papyri themselves. Again, we have incorporated numerous translations of various papyri documents, even at the risk of overloading the treatise. This feature was born of the desire to furnish positive authority for the facts discussed and to enhance the information given by supplying the direct testimony of these immediate witnesses who are so well qualified to speak for themselves. The sources from which these citations have been drawn are fully set forth in a very ample scheme of reference notes. These notes are numbered seriatim by chapters. Cross-reference is thus made possible with the table of references which affords help by indicating at a glance the date of the papyrus document cited. By this means the reader will be able to appreciate more fully their relation to the period of this survey. Other tables in the appendix are for the purpose of giving similar aid in the understanding of this presentation, as well as the pursuit of further study beyond this introduction to the field.

This study first appeared as a dissertation in candidacy for the degree of Doctor of Theology in the department of New Testament interpretation in Southwestern Baptist Theological Seminary, 1930. At the time of its appearance, the author was encouraged by his major professor, H. E. Dana, to submit it for publication. That encouragement was renewed frequently until the death of Dr. Dana. The work of revising the material and bringing it up to date for publication has been done by Dr. Ray Summers, successor to Dr. Dana as professor of New Testament in Southwestern Baptist Theological Seminary.

The study has quickened within the author a zest for further discoveries and has infused into the New Testament even a more abundant significance. It is sent out with the hope that by its use others may receive the same help in understanding of and appreciation for the New Testament—the greatest book in the literature of men.

E. D. HEAD

Forth Worth, Texas

INTRODUCTION

For CENTURIES the hand of God prepared streams of influence which converged in Palestine in the first century of Christian history. Thus it was that "in the fulness of time" there appeared in this little country at the crossroads of civilization one who was destined to influence the world to its most remote corner. The story of this Jesus of Nazareth is told in the New Testament: his virgin birth, his sinless life, his vicarious death, his victorious resurrection, his glorious ascension, his work through his representatives on earth as, beginning in Jerusalem, they spread the "good news" out to the nations.

This New Testament is written in Koiné Greek—the most expressive language known to man. Receiving its stimulus from the Alexandrian conquests, the Greek language took possession of the land which we know in the New Testament period as the Roman Empire. Avid with his appreciation of the Greek language and culture, Alexander the Great saw to it that this language became universal in its use. The Greek in which the New Testament is written is called Koiné, which is itself a Greek word meaning "common." Temporally it is postclassical. In character it is the language of the common people of the day and was nondialectical. The Greek of the New Testament varies from the semiliterary Koiné of Luke, approximating classical style, to the nonliterary Koiné of Revelation, that used by the masses. In between these two extremes will be found the remainder of the New Testament books with varying degrees of style.

This language is characterized by the freshness and vigor of everyday living. As is true of all vernaculars, Koiné Greek was partial to living and vivid expression. This vividness is to be observed in the futuristic present, the use of the present tense to set forth a future action with the reality of a present action, and the historical present, the use of the present tense to present a past action with the reality of a present occurrence. Combined with this effort at vivid expression there is a characteristic simplicity about the language. The style is heavily paratactic, abounding in the use of co-ordinate clauses introduced by the conjunction "and." These and many other elements mark the language as distinct from classical Greek. For many years, students of the New Testament looked upon this Greek as though it were some special language given of God for the sole purpose of presenting his revelation. It remained for the archaeologists to discover the material which would prove that this was the common language of the people in the New Testament day. This fact makes the significance of the New Testament even more striking; God gave his revelation to men in the language which they used and could best understand.

This material was an abundance of papyri collections. The collections on which the ensuing pages are based were discovered in Egypt. It is therefore but natural that the thoughtful student should inquire into the problem of their geographical limitations. Since these widely heralded documents were confined to an area outside Palestine, it is necessary to establish some link of relation between them and the life peculiar to the land to which the New Testament is chiefly indigenous. This problem is not so formidable as it at first appears. It is the contention of Meecham [1] that there is no disadvantage to the Egyptian origin of the papyri. Strategic centers of early Christian culture were found in Alexandria and in cities of North Africa. In these cities and along the banks of the Nile, large numbers of Greek-speaking Jews settled. In that cosmopolitan environment Christianity took deep root. Thus the papyri of Upper Egypt, mirroring the many-sided life of the common people, cannot fail to convey vivid impressions of the background against which early Christianity should be viewed.

This indicates that the broad basis for the solution of our problem is found in the cosmopolitan character of the New Testament world. The great currents of thought and the leading elements inhering in the life of the people were common property and not limited to any one locality. Deissmann [2] indicates that certainly there must have been differences between the country life in Egypt and Palestine due to the differences in soil, climate, and methods of work; however, the common element in the two lands appears to predominate.

One of the common factors to be found in this period was the imperial form of government bearing the stamp of Roman genius. Although it was not in accord with the policy of Rome to interrupt the fixed forms found in the many smaller communities, it nevertheless left its impress and supplied the impulse to universalism. Egypt and Palestine were under the same emperor. Angus [3] has observed that the acme of cosmopolitanism was reached in the conquests of the Roman armies and the administration of the empire. The foundation of the empire was a protest against the exclusivism and all-Roman policy of the oligarchy. The whole world united into a brotherhood and under the rule of a single individual was the dream of Julius Caesar. To a war-weary world, the Roman Empire brought peace, and commenced with characteristic energy the task of consolidation of the many provinces.

Another factor, even more conducive to universalism, was the spread of the Koiné Greek. Rapidly it became the universal language of the eastern part of the empire and was well known even in Rome and all of Italy. This language and culture penetrated to the very heart of Palestine and into its capital, the Holy City. On every side Palestine was bordered by Greek towns. Within it were great Greek centers: Samaria, Tiberias, Caesarea Philippi. Great commercial highways traversed the country from north to south and from east to west. In Egypt, Asia Minor, Cyrene, and Crete, the Jews spoke Greek almost exclusively. It was this general prevalence of this language which gave to the Septuagint so popular and widespread usage. The papyri have proved conclusively that our New Testament was written in the same common language which they employed and which was also intelligible in Palestine and contiguous territories. Thus we find that the barrier of the local dialects was removed and a medium of communication provided which encouraged contact with all sections of the world.

The long and close connection of Egypt with biblical history and life is significant. Omitting Old Testament references, abundant proof can be found in the New of continuous intercourse between Palestine and Egypt. Mason [4] discerningly reminds us that the Light of the world, though cradled in Bethlehem, was taken to Egypt to escape the wrath of Herod. Again, at the close of his life, Egypt entered the picture when Simon of Cyrene helped to bear the cross of Christ. At Pentecost there were representatives of Egypt and Lybia. In the early church, Simeon Niger and Lucius of Cyrene were outstanding teachers. The eloquent Apollos was schooled in the Jewish and Christian tradition in Alexandria. One of the most noted converts to the Christian faith was the eunuch who was the treasurer for Queen Candace of Ethiopia. Very appropriately has Egypt been called the clearinghouse of the first century world. Alexandria was the conjunction point for the blending of the Oriental and the occidental types of civilization. However, even if it were wholly impossible to produce positive proof of any direct impact whatsoever of Egypt on Palestine, it would still be necessary to study Egypt because of its position as a well-defined segment of the circle comprehending the life of the Greco-Roman world of the first century.

By comparative study, many of the features reflected in the papyri, descriptive of the ordinary life of the people, are found to be common both to Egypt and to Palestine. For example, the weavers, the fullers, and the physicians are named in the papyri and in the New Testament. Taxation, and its collection by publicans, obtains in both of these written records; likewise centurions, judges, priests, and even robbers are there reflected. It seems that the various trades and professions which employed the energy of the people in these separate countries bear witness to the same prevailing cosmopolitanism reflected in their language and government. We are in the most thorough agreement with Meecham [5] when he observes that the geographical limitations of the papyri are amply compensated for by the immense variety of the contents.

Thus it appears clear that the papyri can fully qualify as unimpeachable witnesses to the life and literature of the New Testament. They add immeasurably to our understanding of the message of the New Testament at many points because they show so exactly the conditions and customs of the day. Any such aid is thrice welcomed by the sincere student of this greatest of books.

CHAPTER I

HISTORICAL RESUMÉ

Pertinent Passages of Scripture

Can the rush [papyrus] grow up without mire?—JOB 8:11.

And the glowing sand shall become a pool, and the thirsty ground springs of water: in the habitation of jackals, where they lay, shall be grass with reeds and rushes [papyri].—ISAIAH 35:7.

And when she could not longer hide him, she took for him an ark of bulrushes [papyrus], and daubed it with slime and with pitch; and she put the child therein, and laid it in the flags by the river's brink.—EXODUS 2:3.

That sendeth ambassadors by the sea, even in vessels of papyrus upon the waters, saying, Go, ye swift messengers, to a nation tall and smooth, to a people terrible from their beginning onward.—ISAIAH 18:2.

Having many things to write unto you, I would not write them with paper [papyrus] and ink: but I hope to come unto you, and to speak face to face, that your joy may be made full.—2 JOHN 12.

The cloak that I left at Troas with Carpus, bring when thou comest, and the books [papyrus rolls], especially the parchments.—2 TIMOTHY 4:13.

THE DISCOVERY of the Greek papyri in Egypt in comparatively recent times has awakened the most widespread interest. Results are being realized from the study of these almost countless documents which are well-nigh revolutionary. They are focusing their revealing light on the leading phases of biblical research, making possible the most scientific conclusions on linguistic and historical problems which have baffled scholars for the long centuries. It is therefore in order to present a historical resumé of the essential facts included in this alluring field of investigation.

Our first inquiry is concerned with the origin of the papyrus material. We find that it was derived from the papyrus plant *(Cyperus papyrus)*.[1] At the present time it may be found in the Upper Nile regions, in Abyssinia, in Sicily, particularly in the vicinity of Syracuse, and also in Lake Trasimene. The etymology [2] of the name used to designate this plant is as yet in doubt. However, the Greek title πάπυρος (Latin, *papyrus*) appears to be of Egyptian origin.[3] The question has been raised by De Lagarde [4] as to whether the article manufactured at Bura on Lake Menzaleh, of which the Egyptian name was *pa,* was papyrus. Bondi [5] has suggested the derivation from the Egyptian pa-p-yor, "the product of the river," or "river plant." Herodotus [6] always called it βύβλος. Apparently the suggestion of Bondi more nearly describes the nature of the plant, for we know it to be a marsh or water plant, especially prolific in Egypt in ancient times.

Theophrastus,[7] who has supplied the first accurate descripiton of the plant, gives a surprising list of its manifold uses. The garlands for the shrines of the gods were often made from the head of the plant. The root, which was the thickness of a man's wrist and fifteen to twenty feet in length, was used in the manufacture of different utensils, as well as for fuel. From the stem, in addition to the writing materials, boats, sails, mats, cloth, and cords were made. Its pith was a common article of food, and was eaten either raw or cooked. Herodotus corroborates its consumption as food, and incidentally mentions the fact that it provided the material of which the priests' sandals were made. There is considerable uncertainty, however, as to whether the *Cyperus papyrus* could have sufficed for all the uses delineated here. It seems far more reasonable to conclude that several plants of the genus *Cyperus* were comprehended under the name βύβλος or πάπυρος. This view finds support in Strabo,[8] who makes reference to both the inferior and the superior qualities of papyrus. The *Cyperus dives* which is now grown in Egypt is yet employed for many of the purposes enumerated by the ancient authors.

The point of most commanding interest is the widespread use, throughout the ancient world, of the writing material manufactured from this papyrus plant. As the classic writing material of the Wonderland of the Nile, papyrus has a history of roughly four thousand years. Many creditable witnesses lend their very convincing testimony to the attestation of this fact: early writers, documents, sculptures. The ancient Egyptian wall paintings depict papyrus rolls. There are also extant rolls which carry us far back into shadowy antiquity to prove the employment of papyrus materials in writing. Accounts [9] of King Assa (3580-3536 B.C) are contained in the oldest Egyptian papyrus now known. The earliest literary papyrus, designated as the Prisse papyrus, preserved in Paris, has been estimated as dating from approximately 2500 B.C., and contains a work composed in the reign of a king of the fifth dynasty. The Assyrians were also acquainted with papyrus, and called it the reed of Egypt. Proof of the use of papyrus among the Greeks is at hand in a reference of Herodotus, which mentions its introduction among the Ionian Greeks. It seems that they gave it the name διφθέραι (skins), because they were already accustomed to this sort of material. Very dependable evidence [10] convinces us of the use of papyrus in Italy, but the information necessary to enable us to fix the exact date is wanting. Finegan [11] is confident that it was in use here in the third century B.C., and it is probable that its use started even before that date. The Arabs cultivated and manufactured papyrus for writing materials down to the eighth and ninth centuries, when the demand for it declined because of the growth of the paper industry. This type of writing material became so popular among the ancient nations that its production was the chief article of commerce in Egypt, and Alexandria was its principal center. Indeed, when the Egyptian manufacture of papyrus was at its greatest commercial height, it had become a monopoly, and each leaf had to be marked with a stamp to maintain its authenticity and value.

The Scriptures come in also to add the weight of their testimony to the importance of the papyrus material in ancient times. The plant is named in the passages previously cited. Incidental reference is made in Job 8:11 and Isaiah 35:7. Small boats of papyrus are mentioned in Exodus 2:3 and Isaiah 18:2. The author of 2 John 12 doubtless refers to a sheet of papyrus in his use of χάρτης, and Paul, in 2 Timothy 4:13, certainly has in mind papyrus rolls when he speaks of τὰ βιβλία.

The popular demand for papyrus writing material and its almost universal use arouse our curiosity as to the method of its preparation and processing. For information on these points, we are mainly dependent on the account of Pliny.[12] According to the facts gleaned from this source, the white cellular pith (βύβλος) of the long, triangular papyrus stalk was stripped of its bark or rind and sliced into thin strips. One layer of these strips was then placed at right angles to and on top of another layer. They were pasted together with the aid of Nile water, which was of sufficient adhesive quality, then dried and smoothed. When pressed together, the layers formed a single web or sheet (κόλλημα).[13] A smooth surface was effected by carefully rubbing the product with ivory or a smooth shell. The side of the sheet most desirable for writing was that on which the fibers had been arranged horizontally. This was technically designated *recto;* the reverse side, where the fibers were in vertical position, was called *verso.* The *verso* was used only if one was pressed for space and had matters of importance which had to be presented. Frequently papyrus sheets reveal that once they had been official documents of which the original writing was crossed or washed out and a private letter or a schoolmaster's writing lesson for his pupil was written over the effacement. The size and character of the papyrus sheets varied. For nonliterary documents a very common dimension was five or five and one-half inches in width and nine to eleven inches in length. The sheets were often joined together to form a roll of the desired length. A roll of twenty sheets was apparently common size for selling purposes. Exact information as to the price of the papyrus sheets is not now accessible. There is record of an inscription which indicates that in some instances two sheets cost a little over a δηνάριον (seventeen cents). This may or may not be representative.

One of the most arresting parts of the history of the papyri is the story of the discovery of the papyrus documents which have survived from the ancient world. The collection brought to light consists of a large number of Demotic, Coptic, Arabic, Latin, Hebrew, Greek, Persian, and old hieroglyphic papyri. Of all these, the most valuable to the student of the New Testament is the prodigious group of Greek papyri. Although there are numerous classical fragments among them, the great bulk are of a nonliterary character. The list is extensive: legal documents, leases, accounts, receipts, wills, marriage contracts, attestations, official edicts, petitions for justice, judicial procedure, taxes, letters, notes, exercise books, charms, horoscopes, diaries, etc. The contents of these nonliterary fragments are as varied as life itself. The Greek fragments, numbering many thousands, embrace a period of more than a thousand years. The oldest go back to the Ptolemean times (c. 325 B.C.); the most recent extend into the Byzantine period (c. A.D 640). Frequently these papyri fragments have been found clutched in the hand or swathed with the bodies of mummies.

The first discovery of Greek papyri was made in Europe in 1752 on the site of Herculaneum, near Naples. The excavations yielded a number of charred rolls of a literary character. Subsequent to this initial find, we owe all other discoveries to Egypt. It was not, however, until 1778, at Gizeh, that the first find of

Greek papyri in Egypt was achieved. This was the result of the work of some native diggers whose discoveries totaled forty or fifty rolls, only one of which was preserved. More than forty years passed before anything of significance appeared. But in 1820 a group of documents of the second century B.C. was found on the site of Serapeum at Memphis. Then there followed a period of thirty years of discovery in which several important literary papyri were secured.

The most fruitful season of discovery was the last quarter of the nineteenth century and following. During this time four epoch-making discoveries occurred. The *first* of these came in 1877, when a great mass of papyri was found on the site of Arsinoe in the Fayum. Earlier Arsinoe had been called Crocodilopolis. This Fayum territory is about eighty miles southwest of modern Cairo. It is the site of an ancient submerged lake from which (*Piom*) it derives its name. It was a center of worship for the crocodile god, Sebek. The papyri discovered here were chiefly nonliterary and in very fragmentary state, belonging to the Byzantine period (A.D. 284 to A.D. 640). The *second* discovery of this series was made in 1892 on the site of a village named Soconopaei Nesus. The documents were of the Roman period (30 B.C to A.D. 284), most of them ranging from A.D. 150 to A.D. 200. The *third* and *fourth* great finds, which are the most important of all, are to be credited to two of the greatest pioneer workmen in the field of papyrical discovery, Grenfell and Hunt, of Oxford University. It was during the seasons of 1896-1897 and 1905-1906, respectively, when they were excavating, for the Egypt Exploration Fund, at Behnesa, the ancient Oxyrhynchus, that the events took place. Oxyrhynchus, only about ten miles from the Nile, was the capital of the district during the fourth and fifth centuries A.D., and is marked by numerous churches and monasteries, indicating that Christianity had taken root there at an early date. The thousands of papyri which were recovered here include a number of non-literary rolls, in good condition, and comprise also a great store of fragments of literary works, fragments of the Scriptures, and portions of the writings of various classical authors. This collection ranges from the second century B.C. to the seventh century A.D. One of the most interesting fragments is that which contains a collection of the "Sayings of Our Lord." Some of the sayings are from our canonical gospels; others are not recorded elsewhere. The fragment is dated about the beginning of the third century A.D. and reveals the kind of collection of Jesus' sayings which was in circulation among the Christians in Egypt at that time.

Finds of no inconsiderable importance, supplementary to the four great groups just reviewed, are: Fayum towns (1900), Hibeh (1906); Tebtunis (1902, 1906). The most interesting of these lesser groups is

that extracted by Flinders Petrie, in 1889-1890, from
a set of mummy cases found in the Necropolis of
Gurob in the Fayum. Workmen were engaged in
exploration for papyri. They were working in a
crocodile cemetery where sacred crocodiles had been
buried in religious ceremony. They became discouraged to the point of disgust, as in their search for
papyri they turned up crocodile mummies only. One
of the workmen, his disgust beyond the power of
restraint, hurled one of the sacred mummies to the
earth, where it broke into pieces. To their amaze-
ment they found that it, as well as many others, was
stuffed with rolls of the papyri which they were seeking. In addition to miscellaneous documents, there
are included remains of registers of wills entered
from time to time by different scribes and thus af-
fording a variety of handwritings for study. Further,
the value of the collection is enhanced by the presence of fragments of the *Phaedo* and *Laches* of Plato,
the lost *Antiope* of Euripides, and other classical
works. The last decade of the nineteenth century
was also distinguished by the recovery of several literary works of great importance, inscribed on papyri
which had been deposited with the dead, and had
consequently remained in almost perfect condition.

When due evaluation is given to the foregoing
facts, we may conclude that it is practically impossible to exaggerate the value [14] of the papyri documents. For the paleographer, they furnish concrete

evidence for the study of the various forms of writing and the history of book production. To the general historian, they bring myriads of contemporary documents to make possible the writing of scientifically accurate history of the Greco-Roman times. In truth, according to Baikie,[15] the whole many-colored pattern of human life so many centuries ago unrolls itself before us as we read, and we realize, as formal history could never teach us, that the men and women of two thousand years ago were of the same flesh and blood with ourselves, and that all the great changes which have come in the intervening years have not affected the essential man, who was then very much what he is now. These plain, unpretentious bits of papyrus come as a stream of warm new blood to reanimate the history of law in the first place, but also the history of civilization in general, and of language in particular.

In addition to these general contributions, the papyri supply very specific aid for the Bible student. To him they present a threefold information: First, from the linguistic and philological standpoint, they demonstrate the fact that the language of the New Testament is largely the colloquial Greek, which was the instrument of communication in the common life of the people of the time. Second, we are led to a more vivid appreciation of the style of New Testament literature. Even a casual examination of the artless papyri letters reveals the same basic structural form as that of the letters of Paul. We find, too, that the great apostle was clothing his majestic thought in the everyday words of the people and his epistles in the more informal and nonliterary dress of the popular letter. Third, we are enabled to reconstruct the world of the New Testament and thus catch a comprehensive view of the social, economic, political, and religious background of the life of early Christianity and so determine the leading elements of the soil in which it grew.

Therefore, it becomes our well-defined task to glean from the original sources before us those facts which are sufficient for the illumination of New Testament life, language, and literature.

CHAPTER II

THE NEW TESTAMENT DOCUMENTS

Pertinent Passages of Scripture

And there was delivered unto him the book [roll] of the prophet Isaiah. And he opened the book [roll], and found the place where it was written, The Spirit of the Lord is upon me.—LUKE 4:17-18.

And there are also many other things which Jesus did, the which if they should be written every one, I suppose that even the world itself would not contain the books [rolls] that should be written.—JOHN 21:25.

See with how large letters I write unto you with mine own hand.—GALATIANS 6:11.

The cloak that I left at Troas with Carpus, bring when thou comest, and the books, especially the parchments.—2 TIMOTHY 4:13.

I had many things to write unto thee, but I am unwilling to write them to thee with ink and pen.—3 JOHN 13.

And I saw in the right hand of him that sat on the throne a book written within and on the back, close sealed with seven seals.—REVELATION 5:1.

THE RECENT discoveries of papyri have served with pronounced effect in bringing about a more intelligent understanding of various salient features of the New Testament documents. Perhaps of primal importance is the knowledge they afford of the material on which the New Testament manuscripts were written and the original textual form in which they existed. At last we have reasonable positive evidence of the fact that they were inscribed on real papyrus sheets. Kenyon [1] recognizes this and explains the reason for it. Skins, which might be used for writing material for the purposes of public services in the synagogue, would be too cumbrous for books intended for free circulation, especially for letters. Vellum as a writing material did not come into general use until two or three centuries after the New Testament documents were written. From contemporaries we know that in Egypt, Greece, Rome, and Palestine, papyrus was the material universally employed in writing. The New Testament writers were very likely acquainted with parchment also (2 Timothy 4:13), but this was less commonly used than papyrus.

The actual writing was done with a reed pen, which was dipped in ink made of soot and gum (3 John 13). The sheets of papyrus are said to have measured approximately five by eleven inches in size. The writing was arranged in columns two or three inches wide, separated by small margins. The number of columns depended on the width of the sheet of papyrus; however, there were never more than four columns, and two were common. In writing Greek, the scribe would write first the column on the left and continue to the right. No spaces were left between the words in a line, and no punctuation marks were used. For all practical purposes the Greek letters would be arranged as the English letters are arranged in the following verses from Mark's Gospel:

thebeginningofthegospelofJesusChristthesonofGodasitis writtenintheprophetsbeholdisendmymessengerbeforethy facewhichshallpreparethywaybeforethee

The reader of the fine Greek New Testament or English New Testament owes a tremendous debt of gratitude to the textual critics and other scholars who have simplified the page for our use.

A papyrus roll consisted of a number of sheets, sometimes twenty or more, bound with a thread and sealed with wax (Revelation 5:1). For their security and preservation, rolls were fastened together and put away in arks or chests. The length of a roll would depend somewhat on the width of the columns and the size of the letters. The individual New Testament books represented rolls of varying length. For example, it has been estimated that Mark would constitute a roll nineteen feet long, Romans eleven and one-half feet, while 2 Thessalonians could be written in a four-column roll fifteen inches in length. In the act of reading, the reader would unroll with his right hand and roll up with his left hand what was read.

The title of a book would be given at the end of the roll, on a separate slip fastened at the top.

The discovery of papyri texts has caused the literary character of the New Testament writings to be subjected to a most rigid scrutiny. A comparative study proves that they exhibit the vernacular Koiné, the common language of the everyday people of the time. Hence are the books of the New Testament to be classed as literature in the technical or classical sense?

It appears that the answer to this question is dependent on two points of view: an adequate definition of literature, and a clear conception of the various forms in which it may find expression. As to the first of these, Deissmann [2] looks upon literature as that which is written for the public and cast in a definite artistic form. The books of the New Testament meet the requirements of this definition. As to the second view, the papyrus documents reveal a variety of forms in literary expression. They render aid as nonliterary texts by teaching us that not everything which is written, or which has come to us in written form, is to be regarded straightway as literature. They render aid as popular texts by teaching us that within the department of literature we must distinguish between what is literary and popular and what is literary and professional. Even a casual reading is enough to convince us that the nonliterary papyri were created, not as art for art's sake, but by the very necessities of life. They were not destined for the public and for future generations, but for the routine round of a man's life day by day. It is in this that we find their precise charm. They are the documents of human life, not intended for our eyes, but placed in our hands by a kind Providence who wished to bring us of a later generation into human touch with the olden time.

When the New Testament is measured by the literary norm of the contemporary documents, it is quite generally agreed that only three of its authors approach the level of pure literary style [3]—the author of Luke and Acts, the author of Hebrews, and Paul in part. Luke, who is counted the most literary of all the Gospel writers, uses 750 words, many of which are technical medical terms.[4] There is a literary flavor about his work not found elsewhere in the papyri. The Epistle to the Hebrews is characterized by a studied literary style. Its vocabulary, like its style, is less like the vernacular Koiné than any other book in the New Testament. Of eighty-seven words which are found in the Septuagint and in this book alone in the New Testament, seventy-four belong to the ancient literary works and only thirteen to the vernacular.[5] Deissmann [6] observes that in Hebrews we see Christianity stretching its wings for the conquest of culture—the presage of a worldwide future for the young religion. Paul perhaps comes nearest to classical perfection in Romans and Ephesians. So different is the style and vocabulary of Ephesians that many modern critics reject it from the Pauline corpus. Robertson [7] holds that in Romans 8 and 1 Corinthians 13, Paul reaches the elevation and dignity of Plato. Excepting these three, the remainder of the New Testament books are to be classed as popular productions written in the vernacular, the language found in the nonbiblical papyri. Even the Gospels and Acts qualify for membership in this group.

The most pronounced resemblance to the style of these nonliterary papyri is found in the epistolary portion of the New Testament. After citing a number of contemporary letters in illustration of this fact, Milligan [8] makes the pertinent observation that all are constructed on a general model which, at least in the case of the longer letters, embraces: Greeting, Thanksgiving and Prayer, Special Contents, Closing Salutations, Benediction—just the features which in more elaborate form are found in the letters of Paul. This similarity in style has resulted in the effort to draw a distinction between the "epistle," or literary letter, and the individual, or personal, letter. This question becomes the more insistent when we notice that by far the greater number of the New Testament texts claim to be letters: letters of Paul, letters of Peter, letters of John, letter of James, etc. Therefore, shall we regard these as "nonliterary letters" or as "literary letters"? In this connection it may be helpful to consider the opinion that the ordinary let-

ter is a confidential conversation reduced to writing,
which is not concerned with the public and is essentially private. If we indorse this view, the letters of
Paul, for example, are automatically excluded from
their position as forms of literary art and must be
classed as *documents humains,* not written for publication and for ages after ages, but simply for their
contemporaries. Deissmann [9] is the most ardent
champion of the foregoing interpretation, and says
further that the Pauline letters differ from the stores
of private letters recovered from the sands of Egypt,
not "as letters," but as "letters of Paul."

Other scholars of international note dissent rather
emphatically from this distinction advocated by Deissmann. Milligan [10] considers it strained, and in refuta-
tion says that the letters of Paul may not be epistles,
if by that we are to understand literary compositions
written without any thought of a particular body of
readers. At the same time, in view of the tone of
authority adopted by their author and the general
principles with which they deal, they are far removed
from the unstudied expression of personal feeling
which we associate with the idea of a true letter. And
if we are to describe them as letters at all, it is well
to define the term still further by the addition of
some such distinguishing epithet as "missionary" or
"pastoral." It is not merely Paul the man but Paul
the spiritual teacher and guide who speaks in them
throughout their message. Robertson,[11] too, has taken

exception to the position of Deissmann. He holds that Deissmann has given to "literary" a too technical sense. He cites, as illustration of the fact that the New Testament does rise to the height of literary flavor and nobility of thought and expression, 1 Corinthians 13, Romans 8, and Ephesians 3.

In view of the foregoing diversity of opinion, a somewhat intermediate position between the extremes of the literary and the nonliterary appears to be the most satisfactory. Let it be said that the letter-like character of the Pauline productions can be recognized most readily and that some of them are apparently much more artless, informal, and personal than others. They also smack of the local environment which evoked them because they were, without exception, occasioned by some situation or problem peculiar to the several Christian communities to which they were directed. But when we have frankly conceded these points, which the papyri clearly demonstrate, certain portions of the Pauline creations are left which transcend the less pretentious limitations of the everyday personal letter and rise to the standard of the more formal epistle. On the whole, however, not one of them is ever entirely separated from the personal and decidedly intimate matters of the ordinary human contacts. We might add also that dogmatic assertions as to how clearly the apostle Paul comprehended the destiny of his writings in the subsequent history of Christianity will prove to be very wide of the mark. It would seem even more reasonable to assume his consciousness of the immortal character of the truth he was recording and the power of the Spirit inspiring him to give it permanence in the records of succeeding generations.

One of the most revolutionary revelations of the papyri is that which has solved the puzzle of the character of the Greek of the New Testament. Three schools of interpreters have emerged during the years of search for a satisfactory solution of this question. The first of these advocated the theory that New Testament Greek was strictly classical, its supposed peculiarities being discovered in nonbiblical writings. This was called the Purist position. The second school suggested that the idiom of the New Testament was of Semitic cast. The third persisted in the claim that the Greek of the New Testament was simply the vernacular of its own day, the language of ordinary conversation. The papyri and inscriptions have completely vindicated the claims of this third school. Accordingly, it is now quite generally agreed among scholars that there can be no real historical investigation of the language of the New Testament which does not begin with the language found in these commanding witnesses. The papyri and the inscriptions have proved beyond controversy that the Greek tongue was practically the same, whether in Egypt, Herculaneum, Pergamum, or Magnesia. The New Testament uses the language of the people, but there is about it a dignity, a restraint, a pathos far beyond the trivial nonentities in much of the papyri.[12] Cobern [13] convinces us of this truth with his estimate, indicating that of the 5,000 words or more in the Greek New Testament about 3,000 are found in ancient Attic writers. The remainder are almost all taken from the Koiné or popular language of the first century. Only about twenty Hebrew words appear in the New Testament, although it has not been many years since hundreds of terms supposedly Hebraic were acknowledged by scholars.

Hebrew in N.T.

The first to recognize that the papyri were written in exactly the same language of the New Testament was Adolph Deissmann. He published his revolutionary discovery in 1895. The most outstanding opponent at first was Friederich Blass, who later abandoned his opposition. The view has now won almost universal recognition. The colloquialisms and solecisms of biblical Greek are no longer regarded as unique marks of a specially sacred language peculiar to the New Testament. They are now known to be the natural features of the vernacular of the plain people of the day.

The papyri have added new zest to the study of New Testament grammar. The revival of interest in this field is evinced by the publication of eight or nine grammars of outstanding worth. The great grammarians who have done special research under the light of the papyri have shown that the grammar of the Koiné is the grammar of the New Testament. Cobern [14] has furnished a valuable summary of the particular anacolutha of the grammar of the Greek New Testament found in the nonbiblical papyri. His study reveals that in the Koiné of the first century, as contrasted with the classical Greek, old suffixes were dropped, new ones coined, and the number of words compounded by juxtaposition greatly increased. The *nominativus pendens* is much in evidence. The neuter plural is used with either singular or plural verb; the use with singular predominates. The accusative is gaining ascendancy. The comparative form of the adjective frequently is used to express the superlative idea. The use of the personal pronoun is becoming more frequent, but that of the possessive is decreasing. In the verb there is a marked tendency toward simplification. Cases with prepositions are changing. Optatives are disappearing. The instrumental use of ἐν is common. The future participle is less frequent. The growth of the passive over the middle is marked. In lexical study we observe that words from town life (the stage, the market place, etc.) come to the front, and there is a marked increase in the number of diminutive forms. The prepositions exhibit a great flexibility.

To the more general, but none the less vital, problems of criticism, papyri have brought considerable illumination. In the front rank of importance is their service in establishing the science of Greek paleography on a solid basis. They have made it possible by comparative study of the various changes in handwriting and orthography to distinguish a first century Greek manuscript from one of the third century with as much ease as an English manuscript of the sixteenth and one of the nineteenth century can be differentiated. The application of this principle has caused even many of the most skeptical scholars to date the New Testament documents in the first century. Two generations ago the late dates were championed by numerous defenders, but now few have rallied to the support of this position.

Date of N. T. Documents [handwritten marginal note]

The papyri have inspired great confidence and assurance concerning the New Testament autographs. It is at first somewhat disturbing to the student when he discovers that no manuscripts are now extant bearing the actual signature of Matthew or Luke or Paul. The great uncial Greek manuscripts bring us no nearer these originals than the early fourth century A.D. New Testament portions, in Coptic, Syriac, and Latin push the date back into the early second century, as do some of the Chester Beatty Papyri. Although there are slight changes possible from the original autographs, changes in lexical and grammatical idiom, the great uncial manuscripts have retained the ancient and peculiar forms of the first century to such an extent that they are undoubted to the unprejudiced mind. Milligan [15] speaks with confidence at this point in saying that in all substantial particulars the words of the autographs have been recovered. To say the least, the new discoveries make it possible to get back to the original New Testament with more certainty than to any other ancient book. By comparison of the time element involved, we note that classical manuscripts now extant fail by several centuries to get back as near the originals as do the New Testament manuscripts. For example, the best attested manuscripts of men like Sophocles, Euripides, Vergil, and Cicero range from 500 to 1600 years after the originals. Those of Aeschylus, Aristophanes, and Thucydides are 1400 years after the death of the authors; those of Catullus, 1600; of Plato, 1300; of Demosthenes, 1200. These manuscripts number in the hundreds only. The New Testament manuscripts number in the thousands: 1,000 early versions, 4,000 Greek manuscripts, 8,000 Latin manuscripts. Besides all this, much of the New Testament can be reproduced from quotations found in the early Christian writers. Hence, unless the world itself were destroyed, it was impossible for the New Testament to be destroyed. The mass of new discovery has only made more certain the antiquity and essential integrity of the New Testament text, as all the great critics admit.[16]

The knowledge which we now possess, through the assistance of the new discoveries, of the ancient custom of writing books and letters by dictation has served to elucidate several critical questions. There were professional copyists to whom the author would dictate his book. Scribes were regularly employed in publishing books. Paul made use of an amanuensis (first century stenographer) in the production of his letters. Tertius, who is one of them, has given us his name in Romans 16:22. Paul always signed his name at the end (2 Thess. 3:17). Sometimes he would write a section of a letter (Gal. 6:11), while at other times he wrote the whole epistle (Philemon). We find that the nonbiblical papyrus letters were usually written in one hand and signed in another. Hence, Paul and the other New Testament writers were simply following the well-established custom of their time. When, therefore, we are confronted with the differences of style in letters attributed to the same author, it seems most reasonable to explain these differences on the hypothesis of a difference in scribes. This may explain the differences in style in 1 and 2 Peter and the radical difference in style observed when 1 and 2 Timothy and Titus are compared to Paul's earlier letters. Grammatical solecisms, broken connections, etc., are explicable in Paul's letters when the use of dictation is known. This custom accounts also for the vividness of the New Testament language. The author spoke it to an amanuensis, and there was always a definite audience before him, and he was really addressing them through the scribe. The occurrence of lacunae and various forms of textual corruption are almost inevitable when we remember that the originals were written on papyrus materials. This possibly explains the abrupt ending of Mark, since the ends of a roll were subjected to more frequent handling. We can understand more readily now how separate rolls dealing with cognate matters could be joined together as if composed on the same occasion. Many critics find in this the solution to the critical problem of 2 Corinthians with its variety of materials and attitudes of approach.

The facts reviewed in the foregoing pages convince us that it is indeed a far cry from our compact, handsomely bound Bible of the present day to the first-century Scripture roll with no separation of words and no punctuation marks. They show, too, how great is our debt to the papyri documents which have made possible a more comprehensive and intelligent understanding of the textual form and content of the New Testament documents. A knowledge of all these matters is utterly indispensable to a properly gauged criticism of their character and content.

CHAPTER III

PHILOLOGICAL REFLECTIONS

Pertinent Passages of Scripture

In the beginning was the Word, and the Word was with God, and the Word was God.—JOHN 1:1.

If a man love me, he will keep my word.—JOHN 14:23.

The words that I have spoken unto you are spirit, and are life.—JOHN 6:63.

Putting away therefore all wickedness, and all guile, and hypocrisies, and envies, and all evil speakings, as newborn babes, long ,for the spiritual [unadulterated, P. Oxy., VIII, 1124:11] milk which is without guile, that ye may grow thereby unto salvation.—1 PETER 2:1-2.

I would that they that unsettle [upset, P. B.G.U., IV, 1079:20] you would even go beyond circumcision.—GALA-TIANS 5:12.

When therefore thou doest alms, sound not a trumpet before thee, as the hypocrites do in the synagogues and in the streets, that they may have glory of men. Verily I say unto you, They have received [receipt in full, P. Tebt., I, 109:17] their reward.—MATTHEW 6:2.

Knowing that the proving [proved, standard, genuine, P. Tebt., II, 392:22] of your faith worketh patience.—JAMES 1:3.

Yea verily, and I count all things to be loss [bones thrown out on the street to the dogs. Cf. Cobern, *op cit.*, p. 123] for the excellency of the knowledge of Christ Jesus my Lord: for whom I suffered the loss of all things, and do count them but refuse, that I may gain Christ.— PHILIPPIANS 3:8.

Now when they beheld the boldness of Peter and John, and had perceived that they were unlearned and ignorant [private persons, P. Fayum, 19:12] men, they marvelled; and they took knowledge of them, that they had been with Jesus.—ACTS 4:13.

O foolish Galatians, who did bewitch you, before whose eyes Jesus Christ was openly set forth [placarded, or posted up] crucified?—GALATIANS 3:1.

Now these things happened unto them by way of example; and they were written for our admonition, upon whom the ends [toll, P. Oxy., IX, 1200:45] of the ages are come.—1 CORINTHIANS 10:11.

Now faith is assurance [title-deeds, Cf. Grenfell and Hunt] of things hoped for, a conviction [test] of things not seen.—HEBREWS 11:1.

THESE PASSAGES are designated to illustrate the light the papyri throw upon the meanings of words found in the New Testament. Robertson [1] reminds us that while the evidence that the New Testament Greek in the vernacular Koiné is partly grammatical, it is chiefly lexical. Our attention in this chapter is to be devoted exclusively to the latter phase of the subject. The New Testament writers reveal their wisdom in their adoption of the terms familiar to the people which were constantly employed in everyday usage. Their task was not to coin new ones but to enrich old ones. No objection need be taken to the term "New Testament Greek" if by its use it is recognized that the authors gave the vocabulary they found in common currency a new and richer meaning. Everyday words were filled with a deeper content. Ramsay [2] recognizes this element of strength in the suggestion that along with the religious conceptions and the organizing forms, Paul (and in smaller degree the pre-Pauline teachers) adopted the names and words of existing society. He did not attempt to create a new Christian language; such an attempt would have proved vain and would have stultified itself. He spoke to his audience in their own language in order to reach their hearts. The already existing words he filled with a fuller, richer, and more spiritual content. He frequently took a commonly used word and made it carry an additional emphasis or shade of meaning clearly noted in the context in which he used it.

The philologist finds increasing delight in the more accurate meanings now imparted to the New Testament vocabulary by a comparative study of its use in the nonbiblical papyri. Many words hitherto classed as "biblical" or "New Testament" Greek are now found in the papyri employed as vehicles of communication in the living language of that age.

At one time it was calculated that about 550 words used in the New Testament were "biblical." Today, however, Deissmann [3] and others will admit only about fifty words peculiar to the New Testament. He has catalogued [4] sixty-seven words from the New Testament and Septuagint upon which the papyri throw new light. Robertson [5] gives a list of some forty words which were supposed to be "biblical" until they were found in the papyri. He lists [6] another 150 words which, though they had been thought to possess a meaning peculiar to the Septuagint or the New Testament, have recently been found in the inscriptions or papyri. Thayer gives some twenty-five other words common to the New Testament and the nonbiblical papyri, but not found in classical Greek. All this proves convincingly that the vocabulary of the New Testament is practically the same as that of the vernacular of the first century Roman Empire. How rich is its meaning for us! God spoke his revelation of redemptive truth in the terms commonly used and universally understood in the day in which it was given.

In the discussion which follows, there will be cited specific examples of words used in the New Testament which are now known to have been in popular use in the papyri. Such a list of concrete witnesses will do more than pages of abstract argument formulated to establish this thrilling fact. These words are only representative and suggestive. The list is not meant to be exhaustive. It could be supplemented by hundreds of similar illustrations as witnessed by Moulton and Milligan.[7]

LEXICAL ILLUSTRATIONS

ἀδελφός—This word abounds in the Greek New Testament and is translated "brother." It is exactly the same term used for members of the Serapeum of Memphis and other religious associations of the first century. Hence it appears that it does not always refer to a blood brother. Frequently it refers to a fellow associate in religious or social life. Cf. P. Tor. I 1:120 [8] and P. Par. 42:1.[9]

ἄδολος—Translated "spiritual" milk in 1 Peter 2:2, but was found in the papyri with the meaning "unadulterated." Cf. P. Hib. I, 85:16, which refers to "unadulterated" grain. P. Oxy. VIII, 1124:11, refers to "wheat that is new, pure, unadulterated, and unmixed with barley." P. Oxy. IV, 729:19, makes the application to oil.

ἀναστατόω—*unsettle.* Paul mentions in Galatians 5:12 those who are "unsettling" (ἀναστατοῦντες) his converts. The word is very common in the papyri. For instance, in B.G.U. IV, 1079:20 also Milligan's [9] Selections, 15:20, a man who is being driven to the wall in money matters makes the plea, "Do not upset me." The word also expresses the complaint of a mother against her naughty boy when she declares, "He is upsetting me." P. Oxy., I, 119:10.

ἄφεσις—*forgiveness.* It was apparently a technical expression for the "release" of the water from the sluices or canals for the purpose of irrigation. Cf. P. Petr. II, 13:2. A nearer approach to the Pauline use for "forgiveness" is afforded by the occurrence of the word in inscriptions for remission from debt or punishment.

ἀπέχω—*have*. The verb used with μισθόν and found repeated three times by Jesus in the phrase, "They have their reward" (Matt. 6:2). It is found scores of times in the papyri in the sense of "receipt in full." B.G.U. II, 584:5; P. Par. 52:3; P. Tebt. I, 109:17.[10] Paul uses the verb in the same sense in Philippians 4:18.

βροχή—*rain*. In Matthew 7:25, 27, "and the *rain* descended," etc. Cf. P. Oxy., I, 101:25; 280:5; P. Tebt., II, 401:27, where its several forms are translated: "a failure of water," "inundations," "artabae of water," respectively.

βιάζωμαι—*press*. Little help has yet been found for the difficult Logion of Matthew 11:12, "The kingdom of heaven suffereth violence, etc." Cf. P. Oxy., II, 294:16, "I am being 'pressed' by my friends." P. Amh. II, 35:17, "compelled them to go to the threshing floor." Apparently Jesus meant that men of no spiritual discernment or transformation are "pressing"; i.e., trying to force the kingdom into existence as though they would by very act of force set it up.

βαστάζω—*bear*. Cf. Acts 9:15, "to *bear* my name before the Gentiles," and Revelation 2:2, "thou canst not *bear* evil men, etc." Cf. P. Oxy., III, 507:29; X, 1242: 17; P. Fay., 122:6, where it is rendered "to remove," "bearing their own gods," "to carry off," respectively.

γένημα—*fruit*. The spelling with the single ν is now abundantly attested from the papyri. Translated "fruits of the earth." P. Oxy., I, 88:7; IV, 729:36; VIII, 1441:6. Shown in the best manuscripts in Matthew 26:29, Mark 14:25, "the fruit of the vine, etc."

γογγύζω—Translated "murmur" (Phil. 2:14) and is so attested in the vernacular; e.g., P. Petr. II, 9, "The
gang of workmen are murmuring, saying that they
are being wronged." The emperor is addressed:
"Lord, while you are sitting in judgment, the Romans are murmuring." P. Oxy., I, 33: III, 14.

γραφή—writing. Used for the Old Testament, and was the
common legal term for a royal decree which could
not be altered. In P. Hib. I, 78:18, we read, "Write
to me and get the document from Dorion without
me." P. Oxy. IX, 1189:9, "a return of priests."

διαβάλλω—accuse. P. Tebt. I, 23:4, "had been compelled
to complain." Also has stronger meaning of accuse,
"if you learn that A. is going to accuse you about the
copper." P. Oxy. VI, 1158:22. May be used relative
to deception, "and others by deception," VI, 900:13.

δίκαιος—just. The sources throw little light on the deeper
Christian significance of this word. It occurs frequently, however, in current usage, "just measure,"
P. Tebt., I, 11:13; "just rule," P. Rein. 20:24; "duty
to the king," P. Petr. II, 10:27, "duties of marriage,"
P. Oxy. VI, 905:9. On the meaning "right," "justice," Cf. P. Oxy. III, 486:35; IV, 746:9.

δοκίμιος—Translated "the proving" or "proof" of your
faith (James 1:3; 1 Peter 1:7) was found to have the
meaning "proved," "standard," or "genuine." In
B.G.U. IV, 1065:6; P. Tebt. II, 392:22, we find the
phrase "standard gold." So that James 1:3 should
read that true, "proved," faith worketh patience, and
1 Peter 1:7, "what is genuine in your faith may be
found more precious than gold." It was used for the
testing of coins to determine whether they were
counterfeit or genuine.

δῶμα—dome. Cf. Mark 13:15. In P. Oxy. III, 475:22, the

account is given of a young slave who was killed in trying to see a performance of castanet players in the street below, the word is clearly to be understood as the top of the house. It also has the meanings "homesteads" and "house." P. Petr. I, 26:10; P. Ryl. II, 233:3.

ἐλλογάω—*charge.* Used by Paul when he bids Philemon (v. 18) "put down to his account" any loss he may have suffered at the hands of Onesimus. Several papyri give it exactly the same meaning. P. Ryl. II, 243:11; P. Grenf. II, 67:18; Milligan's *Selections,* 45:18.

ἐπίσκοπος—*bishop.* Deissmann [10] has fully illustrated the pre-Christian use of this term from the inscriptions. In the papyri we may note P. Petr. III, 36, the words "in the presence of the appointed *supervisors.*" P. Oxy. VI, 903:15, an accused husband is said to have made a certain statement on oath, "in the presence of the bishops and of his own brothers."

εὐχαριστέω—Originally, "do a good turn to," "oblige." P. Petr. II, 2, (4) 6. In late Greek it passed into the meaning "be grateful," "give thanks." P. Tebt. I, 56:9, "I immediately gave thanks to the gods that you were well." Note the frequent recurrence of the Pauline εὐχαριστῶ τῷ θεῷ μου.

ζημία—Translated "loss" in Philippians 3:7, 8; Acts 27:10, 21. A papyrus uses this same word for the bones thrown out on the street to the dogs. Cf. Cobern,[11] *op. cit.,* p. 123.

ἡλικία—*length of life.* The only New Testament passages where the word must mean "stature" are Luke 19:3 and Ephesians 4:13. The word is very common in the papyri for age, and is frequently used in such phrases as being "under age" or coming "of age,"

which in Egypt took place at the age of 14. P. Ryl.
256:4; P. Oxy. II, 247:13. In Matthew 6:27, then,
Jesus appears to have "age," not "height," in mind
when he rebukes the people for anxiety over the
provisions for the body—"Who of you by anxiety
can add a few years to your life?" Modern science
has demonstrated that anxiety has the opposite effect!

θεμέλιον—*foundation*. The neuter, τὸ θεμέλιον, can be seen
in P. Petr. II, 14 (3):2, "for drying the foundation";
III, 46 (4) 4, "to those who dug the foundation."
Compare Acts 16:26, which tells how the "founda-
tions" of the prison were so shaken by the earth-
quake that the building was broken up and the pris-
oners made free.

θεωρέω—*see*. P. Tebt. I, 58:25, "Seeing me in daily attendance he has as it were turned coward." Hardly
a synonym for ὁράω. Cf. the use of the two verbs in
John 16:16. In P. Oxy., I, 33-3:9, read, "Behold one
led off to death." It is closely related to θεάομαι—to
gaze upon a spectacle—the word from which we de-
rive the English theater.

ἰδιώτης—In P. Fay. 19:12, "a *private* person," and in P.
Oxy. XII, 1409: 14, we read of overseers chosen
"from magistrates or private persons." P. Ryl. II, iii
(a):17, a census return, "a private person paying
poll tax." P. Tebt. II, 381:18, used of "private
debts." Used of a "private" in the sense of absence
of military rank in P. Hib. I, 30:21. Cf. 1 Corinthians 14:16, 23 and 2 Corinthians 11:6.

ἱλαστήριος—*propitiation*—Evidence proves that in nonbiblical papyri and inscriptions this word was used
in the adjectival sense—"of use for propitiation." P.
Fay. 337, 1:3. The related word ἱλασμός (1 John 2:2)

was in the sense of a propitiatory gift. These are pertinent suggestions as we approach the theological implications of the word ἱλαστήριος in Romans 3:25.

καθαρός—*clean*. This word, with its derivatives, has a wide range of use, being applied physically to animals, land, grain, bread, milk, etc.; e.g., B.G.U. IV, 1018:25; P. Oxy., VIII, 1124:11; IV, 736:26.

Κύριος Ἰησοῦς—*Lord Jesus*. The emperors when deified (first century and later) were addressed as "God," "Son of God," "Lord," "Saviour of the world," etc. This gives new point to the use of the titles for Jesus. We see now that Κύριος Ἰησοῦς was an ascription of deity to Jesus. If this does not prove the deity of Jesus, it at least shows that the church of the first century unequivocally accepted in full measure the deity of Jesus Christ.

κύριος—*Lord*. Recently discovered papyri speak of Nero as "the Lord." P. Oxy., II, 246:30. It is therefore more evident why Paul insisted that Jesus is "our only Master and Lord" (1 Cor. 8:5-6). The use of κύριος was common in connection with the cult of the Egyptian god Sarapis. Note the words: "Before all else I pray for your health, and I supplicate the lord Sarapis on your behalf." P. Fay. 127:5.

κυριακός—"*the Lord's*," i.e., "belonging to the Lord." 1 Cor. 11:20, κυριακὸν δεῖπνον, "the supper of the Lord." ἡ κυριακὴ ἡμέρα, "the Lord's day," Revelation 1:10, ordinarily meant "the emperor's day." Cf. P. Oxy. III, 474:41, "the imperial revenue." P. Oxy. XII, 1461:10, "in Imperial ownership." The early Christians regarded the first day of the week as belonging to the Lord by virtue of his resurrection.

λογεία—This strange word used in 1 Corinthians 16:1-2 and translated "collection" has been found recently

with the same meaning in some papyri. It was used
in connection with the "tax" or "collection" which
the labor guilds or the government had a right to
make. Cf. P. Hib. I, 51:2, "the copy of the letter
about the collection of [the value of] the green
stuffs." P. Tebt. I, 58:55, "Urge on Nicon concerning the collection." P. Oxy. II, 239:8, "I swear that
I have levied no contributions whatever in the above
village." The editors note that "λογεία is used for
irregular local contributions as opposed to regular
taxes."

μικρός—*little*. Found in Mark 15:40 refers invariably in
the papyri to age, not stature, so that the question
means, "Can one add anything to the length of his
life?" Cf. ἡλικία in this work.

μυστήριον—*mystery*. This important word is used twenty-
six times in the New Testament, ten of which are
found in Colossians and Ephesians. In its technical
sense in pagan religion, it denoted a "secret" or
"secret doctrine" known only to the initiated, which
they are not at liberty to disclose. On the other
hand, the New Testament usage signifies something
hitherto hidden but now revealed.

ὄνομα—*name*. The word occurs in the secular non-Jewish
papyri with the meaning of "person." This meaning
is found in Acts 1:15, Revelation 3:4; 11:13, and
may be illustrated from P. Oxy. IX, 1188:8 in the
translation, "from the person below written." Cf.
also B.G.U. I, 113:11, P. Thead. 41:10.

εἰς τὸ ὄνομα—This phrase is found in many inscriptions
in which slaves are mentioned as being bought by
the temple "into the name" of a certain deity, meaning that the slave mentioned now belongs to God.
Therefore baptism "into the name" or belief "into

the name" meant, according to an ancient and well-known sacred formula, that he was thus officially marked as belonging to God. The phrase is frequent in the papyri with reference to payments made "to the account of anyone." P. Rein. 44:27. Other uses of ὄνομα with various prepositions are: "Carrying out everything in my name and during my absence," P. Tebt. II, 317:32; i.e., acting as he would act if he were present. "Go and see Herodes in my name and say to him." P. Oxy. VII, 1063:3. Cf. New Testament ideas of praying "in the name" of Jesus, etc.

παιδαγωγός—*attendant.* The translation of this word in Galatians 3:24 as "teacher" or "tutor" has led to a misinterpretation of Paul's idea. In P. Oxy. VI. 930, a mother writes to her son regarding his education. She urges that it be his care and that of his παιδαγωγός that they find for him the proper teacher. This with many other references indicates that the παιδαγωγός was not the teacher. He was a servant who conducted the child to the correct teacher. He also exercised watchcare over the conduct of the child. Paul says that the Law was such a παιδαγωγός (attendant, servant). Its duty was to watch over the conduct of men as it brought them to Christ. *He* is the teacher. Martin Luther's failure to observe this usage of παιδαγωγός led him to the interesting and amusing interpretation which he gave to this passage. His interpretation may be quite "human," but it completely misses Paul's thought. He interprets the Law as the teacher and the Christian as the pupil and sets out the existing animosity between them. "Who ever heard," he says, "of a schoolboy who loved his teacher? Of course he doesn't love the one who frustrates his wishes and beats him with a stick. If he were big enough, he would take the stick and beat the teacher!"

προσευχή–*prayer*. In B.G.U. IV, 1080:4, we find a pagan instance of the use of the word in the general sense of "prayer" and "supplication." An example of its meaning as a Jewish place of prayer (Acts 16:13) is found in P. Tebt. I, 86:18. The inscriptions afford instances of its use for a place of heathen worship.

πηλίκα γράμματα–When Paul thus speaks of the "large characters" in which he writes to the Galatian church (6:11), this may be "amiable irony" or perhaps may be a distinct act of respect, since in writing to distinguished persons it is now seen that the chirography was expected to be larger than in ordinary writing.

προγράφω–In Galatians 3:1, Paul refers to Jesus Christ as having been openly "set forth," προγραφῆναι, as crucified before the Galatians. In one papyrus (P. Flor. I, 99:11) a father employs this same word when he speaks of having "placarded" or caused a notice "to be posted up," declaring that he would be no longer responsible for his son's debts, seeing he had squandered his own goods in "riotous living"–ἀσωτευόμενος (Luke 15:13). Cf. also the question to an oracle (P. Oxy. XII, 1477:11), "Is my property to be sold by auction?" and P. Tebt. II, 411:8, "He might even have proscribed you, had I not promised that you would be present today." The word in substantive form is frequent in official and other notices; e.g., P. Tebt. I, 35:8, "Let the following proclamation be published with the concurrence of the komogrammateus."

πήρα–*wallet*. In Mark 6:8, Jesus enjoins his apostles to take "no bread, no wallet, no money." The term for wallet was a beggar's collecting bag which the peripatetic religious teachers habitually carried with them. This is Deissmann's [12] interpretation. In support of this view, he cites an inscription in which a slave of the Syrian goddess tells how he went begging for the "lady," adding, "Each journey brought in seventy bags." Evidently Jesus was warning them against going out in some ministerial garb or making any claim of mendicant piety.

σφραγίζω—*seal*. Found in Romans 15:28 and Ephesians 1:13; means in the papyri to be imperially protected and retained for the imperial use. Seals were set on sacks of grain to guarantee the correctness of the contents, and there was a mark (χάραγμα) containing the emperor's name and the year of his reign. This was necessary upon documents relating to buying and selling. This mark was technically known as the "seal." (Cf. Rev. 13:16-17; 14:9, 11; 19:20, etc.) In P. Oxy. VI, 923:6, "If you come, take six artabae of vegetable-seed, sealing it in the sacks in order that they may be ready." Cf. also P. Hib. I, 39:15, where with reference to the embarkation upon a government transport of a quantity of corn, instructions are given that the shipmaster is to write a receipt, and further, "let him seal a sample," obviously to prevent the corn from being tampered with during its transit.

σωτήρ—*Saviour*. This title was regularly given to the Ptolemies and to the Roman emperors. Thus some vivid light is thrown on John 4:42 and 1 John 4:14. Cf. P. Petr. II, 8 (1) B; III, 20. The designation is further extended to leading officials, as when a complainant petitions a prefect in the words, "I turn to you, my preserver, to obtain my just rights," P. Oxy.

I, 38:18. Similarly in the account of a public demonstration in honor of the pyrtanis at Oxyrhynchus, the multitude acclaim him, "Prosperous prefect, protector of honest men, our ruler!" P. Oxy. I, 41:22.

στίγμα—*mark*. Occurs in the New Testament in Galatians 6:17 only. It is thought that Paul is here referring to a common practice of branding the servants of a temple with the sacred sign which put them under the god's protection. To establish the correctness of this interpretation, various parallels have been supplied. Thus in Herod. II, 113, it is provided that a slave in Egypt may secure virtual emancipation by going to a certain temple of Herakles and having branded upon him στίγματα ἱρά to denote his consecration to the god. A similar statement is given by Lucian de Dea Syr. 59. In 3 Maccabees 2:29, Ptolemy Philopater is described as compelling the Jews to be branded with the ivy leaf of Dionysus. χάραγμα for σῆμα as a mark of identity is found in P. Oxy. XIV, 1680:11. On the whole, accordingly, it would seem best to give the passage a wider and more general reference and to take it as indicating simply the personal relation of Paul to his Master with all the security which that brought with it.

τραπέζης κυρίου—The translation, "the table of the Lord," in 1 Corinthians 10:21 finds added significance when compared with the analogous Egyptian expression concerning their chief duty, "the table of the Lord Serapis," recently discovered on a papyrus. P. Oxy., III, 523.

τέλος—Translated in 1 Corinthians 10:11, "ends." It is a legal word occurring in documents dealing with property, which has "come" to a man from his father. The word is found frequently in a series of wills found among the papyri in an obviously technical sense. Elsewhere in the New Testament (Matt. 17:25) it is translated a "toll." The papyri lead us to believe the better reading in Corinthians to be, "To us the 'toll' of all ages has come as our inheritance." Cf. P. Oxy. IX, 1200:45; P. Cairo Zen II, 59240:7.

υἱὸς θεοῦ—*son of God*. The title θεός was applied to the Ptolemaic kings and the Roman emperors. Augustus is even described as θεὸς ἐχ θεοῦ. The title υἱὸς θεοῦ is also frequently used for Augustus; e.g., B.G.U. I, 174:1. In the imperial oath the person of the emperor is directly invoked. B.G.U. II, 543:1.

ὑπόστασις—Translated "assurance" in the Revised Version. Drs. Grenfell and Hunt tell us it was a technically legal term and meant collection of papers bearing upon the possession of a piece of property. This word may then be translated "title-deeds"— abstract. "Faith is the 'title-deeds' of things hoped for."

φίλος—*friend*. A title of honor given at the court of the Ptolemies to the highest royal officials.

χριστιανός—*Christian*. This term meant originally an imperial slave, or soldier, belonging to the divine Christ, just as χαισαριανός, "Caesarian," meant a slave or soldier of the Caesar.

CHAPTER IV

DOMESTIC RELATIONS

Pertinent Passages of Scripture

Now the birth of Jesus was on this wise: When his mother Mary had been betrothed to Joseph, before they came together she was found with child of the Holy Spirit.—MATTHEW 1:18.

It was said also, Whosoever shall put away his wife, let him give her a writing of divorcement.—MATTHEW 5:31.

Suffer the little children to come unto me; forbid them not: for to such belongeth the kingdom of God.—MARK 10:14.

And another said, I have married a wife, and therefore I cannot come.—LUKE 14:20.

And there he wasted his substance with riotous living.—LUKE 15:13.

And Jesus said unto them, The sons of this world marry, and are given in marriage.—LUKE 20:34.

Wives, be in subjection unto your own husbands, as unto the Lord.—EPHESIANS 5:22.

Husbands, love your wives, even as Christ also loved the church, and gave himself up for it.—EPHESIANS 5:25.

Children, obey your parents in all things, for this is well-pleasing in the Lord.—COLOSSIANS 3:20.

Fathers, provoke not your children, that they be not discouraged.—COLOSSIANS 3:21.

Servants, obey in all things them that are your masters according to the flesh.—COLOSSIANS 3:22.

Masters, render unto your servants that which is just and equal; knowing that ye also have a Master in heaven. —COLOSSIANS 4:1.

SINCE THE HOME is the basic unit and citadel of society, it is ever an attractive theme for the student of the question of vital life relationships. It is encouraging to find that the papyri have not failed us on a topic of such cardinal and primal interest. Indeed, they pilot us across the very threshold of the family domicile and grant admittance into the inner secrets treasured there. Then let us now look through their lenses for a more accurate and vivid portrayal of domestic relations as they really obtained in the Greco-Roman world.

Betrothal and marriage are fundamental in the establishment of the institution of the home. Therefore, we turn first to the facts revealed on these two initial points. Our main information comes from a typical series of marriage contracts written on papyrus and representing regulations touching marriage from some three hundred years before Christ to the fourth century of the Christian Era. Milligan [1] has called attention to the very marked contrast between the stringent provisions regulating the married life of the contracting parties found in the early documents and the extremely mild character of those belonging to the later centuries. For example, the Oxyrhynchus papyri present only a very faint echo of these regulations, and they completely disappear from the contracts of the Roman period. It is a tribute to Christianity that we find them revived and renewed under Christian influences.

The first specimen [2] of these extant contracts which we have examined is dated 311-10 B.C. It has the distinction of being the oldest of its class that has been discovered hitherto, and is also the earliest dated Greek papyrus document which we now possess. For more detailed study we give its translation as follows:

In the seventh year of the reign of Alexander the son of Alexander, the fourteenth year of the satrapy of Ptolemaeus, the month Dios. Contract of marriage between Heraclides and Demetria.

Heraclides takes Demetria of Cos as his lawful wife from her father Leptines of Cos and her mother Philotis, both parties being freeborn, and the bride bringing clothing and adornment of the value of 1,000 drachmas, and let Heraclides provide for Demetria all things that are fitting for a freeborn woman, and that we should live together whenever shall seem best to Leptines and Heraclides in consultation together. And if Demetria shall be detected doing anything wrong to the shame of her husband Heraclides, let her be deprived of all that she has brought, and let Heraclides prove his charge against Demetria in the presence of three men, whom both shall approve. And let it not be allowed to Heraclides to bring in another woman to the insult of Demetria, nor to beget children by another woman, nor shall Heraclides do any wrong to Demetria on any pretext. And if Heraclides shall be detected doing any of these things, and Demetria shall prove it in the presence of three men, whom both shall approve, let Heraclides repay to Demetria the dowry which she brought to the value of 1,000 drachmas, and let him pay in addition 1,000 drachmas of Alexander's coinage. And let the right of execution be as if a formal decree of the court had been obtained to Demetria and to those acting with Demetria or Heraclides himself and all Heraclides' property both on land and sea. And let this contract be valid under all circumstances, as if the argument had been come to in that place wheresoever Heraclides brings the charge against Demetria, or Demetria and those acting with Demetria bring the charge against Heraclides. And let Heraclides and Demetria enjoy equal legal rights both in preserving their own contracts and in bringing charges against one another. Witnessed by Cleon of Gela, Anticrates of Temnos, Lysias of Temnos, Dionysius of Temos, Aristomachus of Cyrene, Aristodicus of Cos.

When these various contracts [3] are brought into review, they are found to possess the following features: (1) definite specifications regarding the dowry to be provided; (2) provision for the protection of the husband and wife from wrongs done by the one to the other; (3) the repayment of the dowry in case of moral default on the part of the husband, with an additional sum as penalty; (4) equal rights of the husband and wife in presenting their charges against each other; (5) a somewhat unusual item is the mention of the bridegroom's father as one of the consenting parties and as surety for the repayment of the dowry in case of a separation; (6) a separation during pregnancy demanded provision of additional money by the husband to meet the expenses of birth; (7) when divorce came to a couple who had children, a part of the dowry was reserved for any child deciding to stay with its father; (8) special provisions in case of the decease of either party.

Of unusual interest in this connection is an extant marriage agreement [4] of the first century, A.D. 36, in which a form of "trial marriage" seems to be indicated. For, the express statement is included to the effect that the marriage of the two parties is not based on a regular contract. It seems, therefore, that a short period of trial was sometimes the commencement of an ἄγραφος γάμος, which period might or might not be concluded by a more permanent contract.

Engagements were ordinarily regarded as binding. But under certain conditions they were broken. We find evidence of this in a formal notice [5] written by a certain John, repudiating the betrothal of his daughter Euphemia to his intended son-in-law, Phoebannon, on account of his misconduct. The lawless deeds of which he was guilty are described as "pleasing to neither God nor man, and are not fit to be put in writing." This document, dated the sixth century A.D., shows how binding the betrothal was and that it was to be dissolved only by formal legal procedure.

It appears that there was the strictest adherence to the terms of the marital contracts. Proof of this is at hand in a record of the repayment of a dowry in a document [6] dated A.D. 58. It reveals a most happy agreement between a wife and a relative of her deceased husband in which the very minute specifications were accorded the most scrupulous attention.

The very high status of marriage in the earlier period is set forth in a most interesting collection of Ptolemaic marriage laws.[7] Unfortunately the papyrus on which these laws are inscribed is so mutilated that only a general idea of their real contents is now attainable. However, the following items have been set down from the collection: The first step prescribed is an announcement on the part of the bridegroom, to some official, of his name, age, etc., and the date of the proposed ceremony. A corresponding announcement was to be made by the bride, acting under the authority of her father. This regulation is followed by a provision concerning the sacrificial ceremonial, for which the ἱεροθύται were responsible; the dowry, on the other hand, was in some way connected with officials called θεσμοφύλακες. Nothing is known of the functions of either the ἱεροθύται or θεσμοφύλακες from other sources. After the announcement of the date of the marriage, certain payments became due. The remaining regulations relate to divorce, in case of which the dowry of the wife was to be returned, the husband being liable to penalties if convicted of having failed to produce it. If the wife was divorced in a state of pregnancy, the husband was responsible for her adequate maintenance and also for that of her child.[8] Enough of this is clear to convince the reader of the lofty conception of the marriage relation which was prevalent during the period when these regulations were in force.

But we must now turn from the discussion of these topics preliminary to the consummation of the marriage vows and prerequisite to the institution of the home, to the consideration of some matters within the home circle.

Our first concern is with the child in the homes of this period. The attention is at once attracted by the notices [9] of birth which occur with considerable frequency throughout the several volumes of papyri examined. The exact object [10] of these notices has not been determined. They have not been regarded as compulsory. They give only the ages of boys ranging from one to seven years. Wilcken [11] has suggested that their purpose was primarily military and not fiscal. If he is correct, this was perhaps a way of compiling the definite register of the potential military strength of a given province. A papyrus [12] dated A.D. 239 indicates that failure to register children does not deprive them of legitimacy.

Very little, if anything, of a definite nature can be found on the play and entertainment of the child.

There is, however, a very singular papyrus [13] of the early first century which recalls the modern alphabetical nursery rhyme and is thought to have been intended for a similar use. It consists of a pair of acrostics and is written in two columns. The first column gives a list of different traders or artificers, each beginning with a different letter of the alphabet from A to Ω. The second column gives in brief sentences the story of a lost garment, the lines of which represent the letters of the alphabet in their order. We give its translation as follows:

Baker, dyer, fuller, spear-maker, oilman, painter, cobbler, breastplate-maker, doctor, locksmith, mason, millstone-maker, shipwright, scraper-maker, armourer, tablet-maker . . . engraver, glassworker . . . goldsmith. . . .

My (garment?) is lost; violent was he [who took it?], well-born was he who took it. It was bought for ten staters; if it had been a cloak I should not have minded. I seek but do not find it. It was taken without cause. He will meet with anger. Just so he took it, my lovely garment. A lion he was who took it, a fool who lost it. It was taken at night. He was a stranger who took it, it was nothing to one like him. I will choke myself, for I am cold. He is indicated to me for he watches me? . . . It is winter, there is great cold. How utterly unfortunate was I.

Is it wild imagination to picture a mother as she lulls her gentle babe to sleep by these rhymes or some child chanting them while at play?

When we inquire into the training of the child, it

is found that all the papyri which have to do with the schools speak only of the boys and do not mention the girls. Only the women of the upper classes were ever well-educated. The poor working girls had no chance at an education. Since the papyri were left us almost exclusively by the common working people, it is not difficult to understand the absence of any testimonial of the education of the girls of this class. A boy (third century) writes to his father: "Do not be anxious about my mathematics; I am industrious." A mother writes to her student son (second century before Christ) extending her congratulations on his having completed his education, saying, "You will have a maintenance for your old age." In another letter a boy's father expresses regret because his teacher (διδάσκαλος) had left him, but gladness because his trusty old servant (παιδαγωγός) was with him and would take him to find another worthy instructor. The British museum possesses many school exercises coming from the second century which still show the hard usage they received from their ancient owners. Some of these contain the alphabet, the order of letters being impressed by a catalogue of familiar names. Then there are syllable lists, each letter being combined with different vowels, and also lists of polysyllables. There are various copybooks in which the same epigram or sentence is copied six or seven times.

In one of these school exercises the student has written at the end: "Good luck to the writer."

A schoolboy's exercise of the third century, written in large sprawling uncials, gives the beginning of a story [14] of Adrastus, king of Argos, and his daughters as follows:

Adrastus, king of Argos, married one of his own rank and had two daughters, Deiphyle and Aegialia, who though not ugly, were unlucky as to marriage; for no suitors offered themselves. Adrastus therefore sent to Delphi and inquired the cause.

There are also the usual puns on the teacher. A rather comical note from a schoolboy urges that his teacher be fed well, so that he may be better natured!

The horrible and shocking practice of the exposure of children presents its gruesome head in the papyri correspondence of the time. A letter [15] from Hilarion, an Egyptian laborer, written to Alis, his wife, June 17, 1 B.C., concerning his own child and a babe probably about to be born to his daughter, reads as follows:

Hilarion to Alis, his wife. Many greetings. . . . Be not distressed if at the general coming in I remain at Alexandria. I pray thee and beseech thee take care of the little child. And as soon as we receive wages I will send them to thee (?). . . . If . . . is delivered, if it be a male baby let it live, if it be a female, expose it.

Consider that ominous word, ἔκβαλε! Note the utter abandon of the author who writes it! Think with what agony and terror it is freighted! Numbers of papyri documents which have come from Alexandria, dating near the birth of Christ, are in reality contracts with women who served as nurses for these little babies picked off the rubbish heap and kept for slaves or used for immoral purposes.

Childish whims keep cropping out in the papyri letters. Here is one [16] which echoes a boy's complaint and keen disappointment very vividly:

Theon to Theon his father, greeting. You did a fine thing! You have not taken me along with you to the city! If you refuse to take me along to Alexandria, I won't write you a letter, or speak to you, or wish you health. And if you do go to Alexandria, I won't take your hand, or greet you again henceforth. If you refuse to take me, that's what's up! And my mother said to Archelaus, "He upsets me: away with him!" But you did a fine thing! You sent me gifts, great ones, husks!! They deceived us there on the 12th, when you sailed. Send for me then, I beseech you. If you don't send I won't eat, won't drink! There now! I pray for your health. Tubi 18.

(Addressed) Deliver to Theon from Theonas his son.

It is easy to imagine the pouting lip and petulant attitude of the childish author of this formidable missile of disappointment. The little letter reflects the meaning of words used in the New Testament in a striking way. "Husks" he calls his father's present which did not please him. So did the prodigal son of the New Testament find unpalatable "husks" to eat. The boy's mother had said of him. "He upsets me." This is the same charge brought against Paul and Silas at Thessalonica—"They have turned the world upside down." Their preaching was disturbing to a world complacent in its sin. One is reminded of Wesley's sermon when a similar charge was brought in his day. The main points were: (1) The world is wrong side up. (2) It needs to be turned upside down. (3) We's the men to do it! Again in the letter is expressed the distracted mother's words, "Away with him!" This was the cry of hoarse throats as men demanded the death of Jesus—rude language, all of it, but exactly the language of everyday life in Jesus' day. Earlier lexicons which spoke of these words as biblical words not found outside the New Testament have been proved erroneous.

There is also the old story of filial prodigality and unfaithfulness. A father is compelled to post a public notice giving warning against the lending of more money to his spendthrift boy. The extravagance of this son is described in the words: "Since our son Castor along with others by riotous living has squandered all his own property, and now has laid hands on ours." [17] A prodigal son [18] writes to his mother confessing all when he says: "I am going about in rags. I write you that I am naked. I beseech you, mother, be reconciled to me. But I know what I have brought upon myself. Punished I have been every way. I know that I have sinned." A father writes a letter [19] of remonstrance to a dilatory son who has left the letters of his father and mother unanswered, and because of whose dilatoriness the father is about to lose a piece of land.

On the other hand are examples of heartful parental concern and anxiety which have their compensation in the manifest love and loyalty of their faithful children. A mother writes her son expressing anxiety for him because he had a splinter in his foot. She continues thus: "Do not then forget, my child, to write me regarding your health, for you know the anxiety of a mother for a child." [20] A soldier [21] writes his father to assure him of his safe arrival in Italy after a stormy voyage, and encloses a picture of himself. A little girl writes to her father in affectionate devotion:

"Ammonous to her sweetest father greeting. Now that I have got your letter and have learned that by the will of the gods you have been kept safe, I have been very glad. And finding opportunity the same hour I have written you this letter hastening to greet you. All yours individually send greetings to you. . . . I pray that it will be well with you." Epicurus [22] writes to a child saying, "For be sure, the reason why both I and all the rest love you so much is that you obey these in all things." There is a letter of a son, Polycrates,[23] to his father in which he expresses beautiful filial concern in the words: "Write to us yourself that we may know how you are circumstanced, and not be anxious. Take care of yourself that you may be well and come to us in good health."

It is quite apparent that love ruled in many homes, in which the families were bound together by its strong ties, but this was by no means general. The shadow of neglect and of mutual complaining lengthens into divorce and complete disruption of the home ties. A letter [24] from a despairing wife to her negligent husband describes the pinch of economic stress which she is experiencing "because of the high price of corn" and expresses censure toward him because he has "never even thought of returning, or spared a look for our helpless state." A complaint [25] against a husband, A.D. 20-50, describes his conduct in the following words: "Having squandered my dowry as he pleased, continually ill-treated and insulted me, using violence toward me, and depriving me of the necessaries of life; finally he deserted me leaving me in a state of destitution." A petition [26] to the centurion from a woman charging her husband with robbery and desertion is vividly revelatory of domestic infelicity: "Several years ago, my lord, I was united in marriage to Hermes son of . . . , of the village of Theogonis, during the lifetime of my parents, and brought him on [the occasion of] the marriage, in accordance with the contract made between us, a dowry amounting to 5000 drachmae. I have also had two children by him and have no thought of another man (?). But he after my parents' death carried off all that was left me by them, and took it to his house at Theogonis and is using it up." A fourth century document [27] gives a very elaborate indictment of a husband who was guilty of the most violent behavior which extended over a long period of time. It appears that he shut up and abused his slaves, tried by torture to make them accuse his wife of theft, hid his keys from her, and climaxed the long series of outrages with the nagging words: "a month hence I will take a mistress." Such offensive conduct was not confined exclusively, however, to the husband. The rash deportment of a wife is depicted in the following: [28] "But she became dissatisfied with our union, and finally left the house carrying off the property belonging to me a list of which is added below. I beg, therefore, that she be brought before you in order that she may receive her deserts, and return to me my property." Evidently the voyage over matrimonial seas was not entirely a peaceful one.

It is therefore not surprising to find the deeds of divorce which bring the separations of unhappy wedded couples to a legal consummation. One [29] of these typical deeds of separation, A.D. 45, between a husband and wife, declares that each renounces all claims on the other, and in it the wife makes due acknowledgment of the repayment of the dowry and superdowry. Its detail of the age and marks of identity of the couple involved is very specific: "Agreement of Pacus son of Paous, about twenty-five years

old, a scar on the left forehead, with his wife Tes-
enouphis the daughter of Onaphris, about twenty
years old, a scar on the calf of the leg on the left side,
etc." A similar deed [30] of divorce, A.D. 96, was drawn
up between a couple who had been married a little
over a year. As in other instances, the wife acknowledges receipt of the dowry, and the husband renounces all further claims upon her. Neither one of
these deeds assigns any definite cause for the separation. However, in other extant documents [31] of this
type, wedded life is abandoned ἐκ τινὸς πονηροῦ δαίμονος,
"owing to some evil deity." The full right of divorced
parties "to marry as they choose without incurring
liability" [32] is recognized.

Even a casual perusal of the matters of domestic
concern delineated in this chapter brings the New
Testament emphasis on each point into the strongest
relief. The sacred page takes on a new glow of meaning and pulsates with the vigor of hitherto unrecog-
nized life in the light of these leaves from the book
of contemporary domestic experiences. The mind immediately turns to Joseph's strict adhesion to the betrothal vows when Mary was found with child of
the Holy Spirit. In contrast to the frequency of divorce and the trivial grounds indicated, recall the
words of Jesus in which he gives only one cause, and
that fornication. Summon also Paul's injunction to
husbands to love their wives as their own bodies. If
shocked by the contemporary letter reviewed in a

preceding paragraph on child exposure, listen to the Master as he says, "Suffer the little children to come unto me, and forbid them not: for of such is the kingdom of God." Of evident appropriateness is the word of Paul enjoining fathers to stop nagging their children. Even the confessions of the prodigal boy are couched in phraseology found in the perennially charming story preserved in the Gospel of Luke. But these points, subject to indefinite multiplication, are enough to show the most skeptical how illuminating the reflections from the unpretentious papyri records are upon the domestic relations indicated in the New Testament.

CHAPTER V

THE SYSTEM OF TAXATION

Pertinent Passages of Scripture

Now it came to pass in those days, there went out a decree from Caesar Augustus, that all the world should be enrolled.—LUKE 2:1.

This was the first enrolment made when Quirinius was governor of Syria.—LUKE 2:2.

And all went to enrol themselves, every one to his own city.—LUKE 2:3.

To enrol himself with Mary, who was betrothed to him, being great with child.—LUKE 2:5.

Behold, many publicans and sinners came and sat down with Jesus and his disciples.—MATTHEW 9:10.

Matthew the publican.—MATTHEW 10:3.

But the publican, standing afar off, would not lift up so much as his eyes unto heaven.—LUKE 18:13.

And when they were come to Capernaum, they that received the half-shekel came to Peter, and said, Doth not your teacher pay the half-shekel?—MATTHEW 17:24.

THE CURRENT documents reveal a thoroughly developed system of taxation, wide in scope, but evidently of great efficiency. When the lines of these hoary records are read, the subdued but ominous murmur of the great masses who are crushed beneath the galling burden becomes increasingly audible.

We turn first to a large number of census returns [1] which extend over a period of nearly two and half centuries. These returns had to do principally with the poll tax. It was at the age of fourteen that males first became liable for its payment, and the obligation continued until the sixtieth year. The amount of this tax varied considerably in the different districts and periods. There were also distinct rates corresponding to distinctions of status. Of four examples of receipts examined in the Fayum [2] collection, two record payments of 20 drachmae, which appears to be the normal amount, while one specifies 16 drachmae. The remaining one of the four is a receipt for two payments on a poll tax account by a slave. Another document [3] cites two successive payments of 12 drachmae each and thus may mean that the tax amounted to 24 drachmae for a year. A receipt [4] issued by the collectors at Tebtunis for the payment of 22 drachmae and 4 obols for poll tax by a priest not only gives a very unusual amount but proves also that priests were not always of the ἀπολύσιμοι, who were exempted from the tax.

The chief value of these returns to the student of the New Testament is found in their periodicity. Enrolments in the provinces of the Roman Empire followed a cycle of fourteen years. The earliest census[5] in Egypt hitherto known is that which was held in A.D. 62. From this date on to A.D. 202 the recurrence of the census at intervals of fourteen years is attested by numerous examples. The papyri make it possible to carry the cycle back to the reign of Tiberius, and with all probability far into the reign of Augustus. In fact, it is reasonably certain that the fourteen-year cycle was in force as far back as A.D. 20. Its existence earlier than this date is not confirmed by any direct evidence, but there is adequate indirect testimony. Indeed, there is good ground for believing that censuses were held for 10-9 B.C. and A.D. 5-6, or in the twenty-first and thirty-fifth years, respectively, of Augustus. In the light of these facts, the historical accuracy of Luke 2:1-4 finds the strongest corroboration.[6] It is clear that Luke, by his reference to the "first enrolment," was implying a series of periodic enrolments, but no extraneous line of proof was obtainable prior to the discovery of these several census returns. From them it becomes necessary to fix the date of the birth of Jesus around 8 B.C. It is also very reassuring to note an order to return home for the census,[7] A.D. 104, which presents an interesting analogy to the Lucan passage and certifies the fact that Herod, when he issued his command, was acting under Roman orders. We are now prepared to appreciate more perfectly Ramsay's avowal[8] of faith in Luke's dependability as a historian when he says that in every case that has been sufficiently tested, Luke has been proved to state, not merely correctly in a superficial and external fashion, but correctly with insight and fine historic sense, the facts of history and of Roman organization in municipal and provincial and imperial government.

It appears that the collectors of the poll tax resorted to the method of dividing their duties among the different members of a group. In an interesting agreement [9] among four collectors, two agree to undertake the collection at the village, while the other two pledged to concern themselves with persons registered at the village but absent from home. Those responsible for the collections in the outlying districts were to pay 1,100 drachmae of silver each month. The two who were assigned to the village were required to "make up the monthly balance of the quota for the poll tax, being responsible for the salary of the sword-bearer." The sword-bearer referred to is evidently an armed attendant who accompanied the tax collectors.

There were other returns besides those having to do with the census. For example we find a number [10] of property returns. It seems on reasonably substantial evidence that these registrations of property were made every ten years. They include cattle, mortgages, and sales.[11] Revenue returns [12] tabulate revenues from properties in corn land and building sites. Every month the tax collectors were required to make returns.[13] They sent in two accounts of their receipts to the strategus. In one of these accounts a list of the individual payments was given, while the other stated the total receipts for each tax.

In exacting the payment of taxes the collectors were also guided by lists [14] issued to them by the government officials. These contained the names of the individual taxpayers, the objects taxed, and the sums to be exacted. The quotas due from different villages were given in lists issued by government officials. These lists were apparently receipted by public officials. There is a receipt [15] issued by the keepers of the public record office at Oxyrhynchus to the *sitologoi* of certain districts of the nome, stating that they had registered in the records various account books of these officials. The collectors sent out notices [16] of the amount due and employed their deputies [17] to facilitate collections.

The publicani were an indispensable cog in the perpetually revolving wheel of the Roman tax system. They are found to be practically omnipresent throughout the provinces of the empire. Their reputation was most unenviable, and on every hand they incurred the antipathy and most bitter censure of the populace. Many of the papyri register frequent complaints against the illegal "bleeding" of these publicans.[18] A petition, dated A.D. 50, to the strategus Tiberius Claudius Pasion from a weaver of Oxyrhynchus makes the complaint [19] that a tax collector named Apollophanes had unjustly "extorted from me among other people 16 drachmae of silver." Another petition [20] from a weaver to the strategus says that the collector of the trade tax imposed on weavers "using great violence seized from me a linen tunic which I was wearing, worth eight drachmae. He also extorted from me four more drachmae, and two drachmae each month during six months." The Jewish rabbis classed these publicans in the same category with robbers and men without honor. In fact, no Jew in good standing was allowed to get money changed from a publican's cash box, since, presumably, it contained stolen property. Intercourse with these men was sternly forbidden as with sinners.[21] The way was ever open for constant abuses and injustices in handling the taxes because the tax on many commodities such as vegetables, clothes, and cattle could not be standardized, and, consequently, the amount of such taxation was left to the judgment of the individual publican. Continuous injustices were also encouraged by the established custom of "farming out" the taxes to the highest bidder. An extant "Sale of Taxes" [22] intimates the difficulty of finding persons willing to take the responsibility of farming certain taxes as follows: "At the last sale of taxes held by myself and you in the presence of the customary officials, the farmers of the tax on sales and the farmer of the tax payable to the record office not only refused to bid, on the plea that they had incurred sufficient loss already, but seemed likely to abscond."

The publicans play a conspicuous part in the New Testament period. We wonder if Matthew and Zaccheus stooped to the questionable schemes of extortion and oppression reflected in contemporary records. Whatever their history prior to their meeting with Christ, his power was adequate to transform them into mighty witnesses for his cause. We are now prepared to estimate the intensity of the Pharisaic arraignment of Jesus for his complete disregard of caste manifest in his associations with publicans. But surely if any group needed his uplifting ministry, it was this particular one. His influence over them was not in vain, for he exalted one to the apostleship and led another to restore fourfold to those whom he had defrauded. In truth, the publicans heard him so gladly that they qualified for entrance into the Kingdom long before the formal religionists who were blinded by extreme prejudice.

But we must now intercept our explanation of the highly developed methods and organization employed for the assessment and collection of taxes in order to mention the wide range of items subject to taxation. From only a casual survey of the table of contents of the papyri, it appears that virtually everything was taxed. It is said that the only business not taxed in Palestine was the fishing industry.[23] Taxes were imposed on religion. "The place of prayer (προσευχή) was taxed higher than the manufactories or 'saloons.' Almost the only business which had to pay a tax higher than these churches or 'places of prayer' was the houses of prostitution. Dr. Petrie found at Koptos a tax report in which seamen were taxed five drachmae, skilled artizans eight, prostitutes one hundred and two." [24] It was the duty of the leading priests in each temple to send in annually to the strategus or *basilico-grammateus* of the nome a list of the priests and an account of the corporate receipts and expenditure for taxes or religious purposes, a γραφὴ ἱερῶν καὶ χειρισμοῦ, as it is called.[25] An impost was levied by the temple of Suchus at Arsinoe, which appears to have been paid on the sale of house property. A 10 per cent tax was apparently collected by the priests on the acquisition of houses or building sites.[26] A tax upon a calf offered in sacrifice [27] has occurred in several published papyri and is explained [28] as an impost paid by the officiating priests upon the profits of the sacrifice. Other explanations comprehend two phases of taxation on sacrificial calves—an impost upon the person who offered the sacrifice and a tax levied upon the priests of one-tenth of the profits obtained by them from calves offered for sacrifice at the Temple.[29] Jesus was familiar with the Temple tax required for the maintenance of the worship at Jerusalem and claimed no exemption from it (Matt. 17:24-27). These various monetary exactions were no innovation, but were accepted as the regular thing by the adherents of the many religions and temples of the time. The financial program executed in the name of religions was enormous.

The different trades and professions were subject to taxation. A receipt [30] for tax on weaving affords proof of the requirement made of the followers of this trade. The apostle Paul doubtless paid such a tax, since he was a member of the guild of weavers of tent cloth. The amounts of the trades taxes varied and were probably levied on the license issued giving authority for the practice of the particular trade. A receipt [31] issued by a certain Apollonius to a mason states that he had paid the required tax on his trade. According to another receipt,[32] 500 copper drachmae were paid as a monthly "contribution" from the millers and fish-salters of Bacchias and Hephaestias. The purpose of this "contribution" is not stated. Several extant receipts [33] refer to a physician's tax for the maintenance of public physicians. This tax seems to have been levied by the state on military settlers. In one instance the tax appears to have been paid directly to the physician.

The numerous activities of business contributed a very considerable portion to swell the coffers which contained the tax money. A beer tax is frequently mentioned. It is believed to be a duty paid by the brewers.[34] A receipt [35] issued to a wine merchant acknowledges his payment of 400 drachmae and witnesses to the fact that these venders of a most popular beverage were required to carry their part of the load. Taxes were assessed on oil [36] of which very little is known save that oil-producing land was taxed. Levies of taxes were regularly made on sales which were technically known as the ἐγκύκλιον and included mortgages as well. Receipts [37] for the tax on the sale of a cow or the acquisition of houses or land corroborate the employment of this tax.

A great variety of other items is represented in the records of taxation. There is the bath tax [38] evidently for the upkeep of the public baths. Land and property taxes are regularly exacted. There are also the pig tax and horse tax,[39] the police tax, and so on ad infinitum. Indeed, it seems that every known object was included in the roster of things taxable.

Yet, in spite of all this detail of taxation from which there was seemingly no possible escape, it is found that certain cases of exemption were recognized. They come under the designation ἐπίκρισις, "Selection of Boys." Kenyon [40] distinguishes two kinds of ἐπίκρισις—one the selection of soldiers for the army, the other the "selection" of boys aged eleven to fourteen for the admission of privileged persons who were exempt from poll tax. There are four applications in the Fayum [41] collection and two among the Oxyrhynchus [42] papyri which lend their witness to this custom of granting certain exemptions.

Thus we see how impossible even in the pages of the New Testament it is for the student to escape the

Argus eyes of the tax system. For it is at hand to clarify knotty problems of chronology, to describe the publicans as real and lifelike in the part they play in its effectiveness, and lead us to a more sympathetic understanding of the crushing load which it imposed.

CHAPTER VI

FISCAL METHODS AND MACHINERY

Pertinent Passages of Scripture

Then wherefore gavest thou not my money into the bank, and I at my coming should have required it with interest?—LUKE 19:23.

And he poured out the changers' money, and overthrew their tables.—JOHN 2:15.

A certain lender had two debtors: the one owed five hundred shillings, and the other fifty.—LUKE 7:41.

And calling to him each one of his lord's debtors, he said to the first, How much owest thou unto my lord?—LUKE 16:5.

The servant therefore fell down and worshipped him, saying, Lord, have patience with me, and I will pay thee all.—MATTHEW 18:26.

And he would not: but went and cast him into prison, till he should pay that which was due.—MATTHEW 18:30.

Even sinners lend to sinners, to receive again as much.—LUKE 6:34.

Owe no man anything, save to love one another.—ROMANS 13:8.

But if he hath wronged thee at all, or oweth thee aught, put that to mine account.—PHILEMON 18.

And when he had agreed with the laborers for a shilling a day, he sent them into his vineyard.—MATTHEW 20:2.

Philip answered him, Two hundred shillings' worth of bread is not sufficient for them, that every one may take a little.—JOHN 6:7.

Why was not this ointment sold for three hundred shillings, and given to the poor?—JOHN 12:5.

A THOROUGHLY informing analysis of the economic and material status of any period is impossible without a comprehensive review of its fiscal system. The era of the New Testament is no exception in this regard, and its students cannot with justification claim exemption from the task of carefully interpreting the financial conditions with which they are constantly confronted in their investigations. The papyri documents now under consideration portray a multifarious fiscal activity and furnish the student of the Scriptures with invaluable information. Indeed, they introduce us to a rather complex but smoothly running machinery for the administration of finance, and many interesting features of the current fiscal methods which were regularly employed present themselves.

It is surprising to find banks functioning with pronounced efficiency. A number of documents have been edited which represent a wide range of transactions in this important field. By way of illustration

we mention three receipts [1] for sums paid into the
royal bank at Crocodilopolis by Marres and two
women, Tamarres and Hierobasis. According to another receipt,[2] some priests paid to a bank a certain
tax whose nature and amount are uncertain. Again
we find a receipt [3] for various sums paid into a local
bank, probably at Euhemeria, by the overseer of
some estates belonging to the corporation of the city
of Alexandria. This is of much importance to demonstrate the degree of development attained at this
time by the banking system. The money paid into a
local bank in the Fayum was to be paid out to a person at Alexandria. This person would naturally not
have to wait for the coin to be actually transported.
The mutual relations and organization of the local
bank and the bank at the capital were such that
money paid into the one could be drawn out at the
other.[4] An order [5] addressed to a banker by a woman
called Aphrodous, requesting him to pay two women,
both named Chariton, six hundred drachmae, supplies further proof of the service rendered by the
banks. We found a banking account [6] listing a series
of receipts, among which are a number of acknowl-
edgments of the payments of taxes. Another,[7] consisting of two incomplete columns, is manifestly an
official account of sums paid or due. The miscellaneous character of the entries in which reference is
made to deficiences in connection with the revenues
from the oil and beer industries and a present from

the state to distressed cultivators, lead to the conclusion that the writer was connected with a royal bank. A short statement drawn up through the bank of Melas releasing Pasion from all further obligations to Heraclides in respect to a sum paid by Pasion into the public banks, proves that releases [8] were made through the banks. We know from a receipt [9] issued by a bank recording the payment of a loan of 3500 drachmae that loans were regularly negotiated by the banks. A mortgage had been guaranteed as security for the loan. Accordingly, in bold outline, all the main features even of present-day banking procedure emerge: viz., deposits, securities, loans, orders for payment, checking, transfer of funds, and releases. We are here reminded of the rebuke administered to the indolent ingrate with the one talent for not committing it to the bankers that it might multiply at interest (Matt. 25:27). His negligence becomes all the more censurable when the wide prevalence of banking methods is known.

Individual and personal loans of varying types and contents were in vogue. Especially unique is a contract [10] in which a husband acknowledges the loan of his wife's dowry. Evidence that loans of public money [11] were made by the official in charge is found in a reference to a deposit from the public moneys which is acknowledged by the borrower. A contract [12] for a loan of 124 drachmae from a woman named Helene to three brothers was consummated at the usual rate of 12 per cent. We are assured from the records [13] of repayment in our possession that many, perhaps the majority, of these loans were faithfully repaid. However, efforts at evasion and indifference to the binding obligations which devolved upon debtors can be easily detected. A copy [14] of a typical loan agreement is followed by a short letter from a certain Tryphon to a friend named Ammonas, requesting him to dun Dioscurus for payment of the debt. Listen to the very modern tenor of this money claim [15] in which the author says, "I suspect the security set up by Theon for the loan has become void owing to a lapse of time," etc. Petitions [16] for relief from debt occur frequently. A petition [17] to a public advocate offers to pay any debt which can be established against the petitioner. Loans were not wholly confined to money, but included grain,[18] corn,[19] and other products of the soil. Repayments in kind were made. The Scripture exhortation, "Owe no man anything save to love one another" (Rom. 13:8), seems unusually pertinent at this point. Our thought turns involuntarily to the man delivered to the tormentors until he paid all because he was unwilling to forgive a debtor who owed him the mere pittance of a hundred shillings (Matt. 18:34).

Sales were regularly executed. A two-thirds share of a grass crop was sold to a priest.[20] This particular share seems to have fallen to the owners of a piece of land which was let out to a group of cultivators who perhaps received the remaining one-third as their compensation for the work done. A young female donkey was sold for 56 drachmae, a price much lower than the costs specified in other accounts. The most careful details are given in the contract [21] descriptive of the salesman, the purchaser, as well as of the donkey: "Mystharion, son of Heron, aged about 40 years, having a scar on the little finger of the left hand, agrees that he has sold to Satabous, son of Pekusis, aged about 30 years, having a scar on the little finger of the left hand, a female mouse-coloured donkey," etc. A contract [22] for the sale of wheat carries us back to the reign of Ptolemy Soter. Real estate deals figured conspicuously in these sales. A house sold in the second year of Nero for 32 talents.[23] A declaration [24] on oath announced the sale of four plots of ground in the Cretan and Jewish quarter of Oxyrhynchus. We find also in this collection very specific agreements touching the sale of a loom [25] and triclinium,[26] respectively. Doubtless James wrote his warning about projecting the plans to buy and sell too far into the future with very concrete examples before him (James 4:13).

Many different methods of remuneration and exchange are expressed in a group of "Orders of Payment." Fifty-five artabae of wheat were paid by order [57] to Posidonius for the rent of a κλῆρος. Two orders,[28] found together, give instruction for the payment of sums of wheat to various persons. An

acknowledgment [29] is made in a receipt for 48 drachmae for the use of pastures, which are evidently
public, whether belonging to the government or to
the imperial private estates. In the same connection
a rather large aggregate of receipts [30] represents a very
comprehensive scale of expenditures. They feature
such items as transport dues, rents on crown land,
nurses' wages, rent of an oil press, share of an inheritance, house and farm rents, salaries, and various
other monetary compensations. The most careful
business methods were employed, and therefore every
transaction involving the use of money or payments
in kind was scrupulously receipted.

The corporate scheme obsessed the business mind.
Corporations of capital, which monopolized every
possible industry and food product, had been general
for hundreds of years, but by the end of the first or
middle of the second century, labor was quite at the
mercy of unscrupulous "trusts," which controlled
prices and the transmission of food products. Even as
early as 191 B.C. a play speaks of the "mountains of
grain" which the dealers had in warehouses; and a
papyrus some centuries later speaks of the high price
of meat as due to the fact that the butchers were in
league with the city fathers. Josephus tells of 18,000
laborers out of work in Jerusalem and, with their
families, in danger of dying, so that the treasures of
the Temple were drawn upon in order to support
them; but this was no unusual condition. Hundreds

of thousands were forced to receive gifts of corn from the state in order to live during the first century. And it was not in every city that the officers acted as generously as in Jerusalem, where the authorities made provision for a living wage for all artisans. In Oxyrhynchus, also, superintendents of food supply were constantly on duty in the second century guarding the distribution of grain so that the people could get bread at a moderate price.[31]

As intimated in the preceding paragraph, the story of economic stress is inseparably linked with the history of financial method and organization. A register [32] of paupers presents an official list of persons described as ἄποροι, who were presumably entitled to relief. These lists were seemingly drawn up for the information of the well-to-do, who were accustomed to contribute to those experiencing financial dearth. The pawn was also resorted to for relief from monetary stringencies. The latter part of a letter [33] from Eunoea gives instructions to a friend to redeem a number of articles which had been pawned. The following letter [34] reflecting money difficulties goes a long way in illuminating the economic situation:

Sorapion to our Heraclides, greeting. I sent you two other letters, one by the hand of Nedymus, one by the hand of Cronius the sword-bearer. Finally then I received from Arabs the letter and I read it and was grieved. Stick to Ptollarion constantly: perhaps he can set you free. Say to him: 'I am not like anyone else, I am a lad.

With the exception of a talent I have made you to pay
my burdens. I do not know . . . we have many creditors:
do not drive us out.' Ask him daily: perhaps he can have
pity on you: if not do you, like all, beware of the Jews.
Rather stick to him (Ptollarion), and so you may become
his friend. Notice that the document can be signed either
by Diodorus or by the wife of the ruler. If you manage
your own affairs you are not to be blamed. Greet Diodorus with the others. Goodbye. Greet Harpocrates.

We draw again from Cobern [35] the striking fact
that much new light has been thrown upon the economic and social conditions among the poor of the
first century. While one court physician in the days
of the Elder Pliny had an income of $25,000 a year,
and a successful charioteer was able to leave his
children a legacy of $1,400,000, and while fortunes
were so common among the rich that Augustus (A.D.
6) laid a tax of 5 per cent on bequests of $4,000 or
over, and numbers of millionaires put up inscriptions
telling of their benevolent gifts, and splendid funeral
monuments on which they show themselves counting
their money; yet the poor were so poor that thousands of them were compelled to go without burial,
thrown into pits like dogs and cattle, while those of
the middle classes, farmers and artizans, were compelled to pay enormous taxes, and when they ran in
debt were compelled to pay 12 per cent, 18 per cent,
and 22 per cent, and, occasionally, 48 per cent interest per annum.

As we have traversed the path blazed by these witnesses to the fiscal methods and machinery, which reflect the economic status as well, we have heard the hum of intensive activity and the babel of voices clamoring for recognition and ascendancy in the busy marts of trade. The world in which Jesus moved was not passive and listless in its business and monetary interests but fully alive to their power and reward. The New Testament itself agrees with the parallel records in its reflections of the pursuits related to buying and selling, the employment of laborers, the difficulty of wage adjustment, the pinch of poverty and hunger. Even one of the most dominant attractions of the messianic hope in the popular mind was the economic release and material prosperity which were anticipated as a sequel to the Messiah's rule.

CHAPTER VII

LEGAL TRANSACTIONS

Pertinent Passages of Scripture

But he said unto him, Man, who made me a judge or a divider over you?—LUKE 12:14.

Agree with thine adversary quickly, while thou art with him in the way; lest haply the adversary deliver thee to the judge, and the judge deliver thee to the officer, and thou be cast into prison.—MATTHEW 5:25.

There was in a city a judge, who feared not God, and regarded not man.—LUKE 18:2.

But if they are questions about words and names and your own law, look to it yourselves; I am not minded to be a judge of these matters.—ACTS 18:15.

Forasmuch as I know that thou hast been of many years a judge unto this nation, I cheerfully make my defence.—ACTS 24:10.

And one of them, a lawyer, asked him a question, trying him.—MATTHEW 22:35.

If therefore Demetrius, and the craftsmen that are with him, have a matter against any man, the courts are open, and there are proconsuls: let them accuse one another. But if ye seek anything about other matters, it shall be settled in the regular assembly.—ACTS 19:38-39.

And when they had tied him up with the thongs, Paul said unto the centurion that stood by, Is it lawful for you to scourge a man that is a Roman, and uncondemned?—ACTS 22:25.

For as thou art going with thine adversary before the magistrate, on the way give diligence to be quit of him; lest haply he drag thee unto the judge, and the judge shall deliver thee to the officer [exactor], and the officer [exactor] shall cast thee into prison. I say unto thee, Thou shalt by no means come out thence, till thou have paid the very last mite.—LUKE 12:58-59.

So the band and the chief captain, and the officers of the Jews, seized Jesus and bound him.—JOHN 18:12.

Then went the captain with the officers, and brought them, but without violence; for they feared the people, lest they should be stoned.—ACTS 5:26.

And if any man would go to law with thee, and take away thy coat, let him have thy cloak also.—MATTHEW 5:40.

Dare any of you, having a matter against his neighbor, go to law before the unrighteous, and not before the saints?—1 CORINTHIANS 6:1.

But brother goeth to law with brother, and that before unbelievers?—1 CORINTHIANS 6:6.

Nay, already it is altogether a defect in you, that ye have lawsuits one with another.—1 CORINTHIANS 6:7.

And sittest thou to judge me according to the law, and commandest me to be smitten contrary to the law?—ACTS 23:3.

And he released him that for insurrection and murder had been cast into prison, whom they asked for; but Jesus he delivered up to their will.—LUKE 23:25.

Now Barabbas was a robber.—JOHN 18:40.

Perils of robbers.—2 CORINTHIANS 11:26.

And where thieves break through and steal.—MATTHEW 6:19.

For yourselves know perfectly that the day of the Lord so cometh as a thief in the night.—1 THESSALONIANS 5:2.

Then are there crucified with him two robbers, one on the right hand and one on the left.—MATTHEW 27:38.

Jesus made answer and said, A certain man was going down from Jerusalem to Jericho; and he fell among robbers, who both stripped him and beat him, and departed, leaving him half dead.—LUKE 10:30.

WHEN WE inquire into the history of empires, municipalities, and nations, we find that not one of them has ever reached solid ground in its advance toward an ideal civilization until its laws have been wrought into a well-articulated code. Until law is clearly defined, there can be no intelligent administration of justice. Therefore, if chaos is to be supplanted by order and harmony, constructive governmental policies are indispensable.

The Roman mind possessed special affinity for law. Wherever the Roman Eagle lifted his proud head in conquest, there law began to perform its miracle of transforming the existent society. Since the Romans brought the world of the papyri under their sway, they are normally expected to reflect efficient means for the attainment of the ends of justice. This they do, as we shall now see.

Regular "Orders for Arrest" show that definite steps were necessary for the apprehension of offenders. All of them adhere to a stereotyped form like the following:

> To the epistates of Tebtunis. Send up Galates and his wife, both children of Cronion, who are accused by Semele daughter of Acusilaus. (Seal) The strategus summons you.[1]

Other orders [2] mention the custom of commissioning a soldier to accompany those arrested and also instruct the local officer who had anything to say in their defense to come along with them. We learn that there were times when the search for criminals was futile by a declaration [3] made on oath and addressed to the chiefs of police at Oxyrhynchus stating that certain individuals who were "wanted" were not in his village or their own.

Official reports run the gamut of quite a wide range of matters requiring legal attention. One [4] of these reports contains the proceedings of Pesouris against a nurse Saraeus for the recovery of a male foundling Heraclas, whom he had entrusted to her care. Incidentally, it is a most forceful commentary on the custom of child exposure and the disposition made of foundlings when recovered. Notice particularly this sentence from the formally arranged report:

Pesouris, my client, in the 7th year of Tiberius Claudius Caesar the lord, picked up from the dung-heap a male foundling named Heraclas.

An extract [5] from an account of a trial in the reign of Hadrian reveals a dispute concerning the ownership of a house claimed by a certain Ptolema. A very interesting papyrus [6] supplies an official summary of an appeal made by the fullers and dyers of the Arsinoite Nome against the exactions, by a minor official, of an undue amount for the tax on their respective trades. Accidents surely did not occur with the frequency of modern times, but a report [7] reflects one which is truly realistic. Information is given in it to the strategus of the death of a slave who had been killed by falling from an upper story while watching an entertainment given by dancing girls. Evidently an inquest was required in such cases because the strategus ordered the ὑπηρέτης to view the dead body in company with a public physician. A similar report [8] contains an order from a strategus to two mummifiers of Oxyrhynchus "to inspect the dead body of Apis son of Pausis, of the said city, and report the circumstances of the case." Essentially the same kind of an order was given to a public physician to examine into the cause of a death which he reports in the following words: [9]

To Claudianus, strategus, from Dionysus, son of Apollodorus, son of Dionysius, of Oxyrhynchus, public physician. I was today instructed by you through Heraclides your assistant, to inspect the body of a man who had been found hanged, named Hierax, and to report to you my opinion upon it. I therefore inspected the body in the presence of the aforesaid Heraclides at the house of Epogathus, son of . . . Merus, son of Serapion, in the Broad Street quarter, and found it hanged by a noose, which fact I accordingly report.

Another [10] of this series of reports gives account of the visit of a public physician, according to official instructions, to the daughter of Aurelius Dioscorus, whom he found suffering from wounds caused by the house falling down. As we enumerate these reports of the calamitous experiences of the daily life, we wonder if a physician held inquest over the bodies of the eighteen on whom the tower of Siloam fell (Luke 13:4).

Official notices were requisite to acceptable legal form. They cover notifications of birth, removal, and death. The notices of birth were addressed to the official scribe. As we have observed in a former chapter, the exact object which these served is as yet unknown. We noted, too, that Wilcken [11] contended that their purpose was a military one, on the ground that the taxes were sufficiently secured by the fourteen-year census, and that only the births of boys were thus announced. Kenyon,[12] however, thinks that this argument loses its weight if, as is now most probable, women were not liable to the poll tax. The following [13] will serve to illustrate their form and content:

To Socrates and Didymus also called Gyrannus, scribes of the metropolis, from Ischyras, son of Protas, son of Mysthes, his mother being Tasoncharion, daughter of Didas, of the quarter Hermuthiace, and from his wife Thaisarion, daughter of Ammonius, son of Mysthes, her mother being Thaisas, of the same quarter Hermuthiace. We give notice of the son who is born to us, Ischyras, aged one year in the present fourteenth year of Antonius Caesar the Lord. Therefore hand in this announcement of the birth. [Signed] Ischyras, aged 44, having no distinguishing mark. Thaisarion, aged 24, having no distinguishing mark. Written for them by Ammonius, scribe of the Nome.

The ordinary habits and customs of the everyday routine are photographed in these notices. For example, a notice [14] from a centurion directs the appointment of "the customary guard." In another [15] all persons who had deposited business documents, such as contracts, wills, etc., in the notarial offices were ordered to appear before the agoranomai and have them completed within a required period of time. This probably means that the provisional contracts had always to be made valid within the first month of the year following that in which they were drawn up. "Notices of Removal" were obligatory when a removal from the place of official registration was contemplated. In one of these the removal is attributed to the lack of means for livelihood. The Egyptian authorities regarded the removal of an inhabitant from his abode with extreme suspicion,

which was no doubt heightened because it was resorted to in the effort to evade taxation. This series
of official documents is climaxed by notices of death.
The value of these is thus given: "To ensure the
proper keeping of census-returns it was customary to
make official notice of all cases of death, that the
names of the deceased persons might be struck off
the lists." [17] A typical death notice [18] is here attached:

To Heraclides, the village-scribe of Euhemeria, from
Mysthes, son of Peneouris, of Euhemeria in the division
of Themistes. My brother Peneouris, registered as an inhabitant of the neighborhood of the said village, has died
in the month Mesore of the first year of Gaius Caesar
Augustus Germanicus. I therefore present to you this
notice in order that his name may be placed upon the
list of the deceased persons, according to custom. [Signed]
Mysthes, son Peneouris, aged about forty-two years, having a scar on his right forearm.

Notices of the death of slaves [19] were also given.

Petitions were well-known and frequently employed instruments to secure legal rights and invoke
the aid of the arm of the law. The following petition,[20] which was made by a woman to the strategus,
brings the charge of assault and robbery against another woman and requests that justice be done:

To Sarapion strategus in the division of Heraclides of
the Arsinoite nome from Tarmuthis, the daughter of
Phimon, vegetable seller, belonging to the village of
Bacchias, at present without a guardian. On the fourth

of the current month Pharmouthi, Taarsenouphis, the
wife of Ammonius, also called Phimon, elder of the village of Bacchias, although she had absolutely no ground
of complaint against me, came into my house and picked
a senseless quarrel against me. Not only did she strip off
my tunic and mantle, but also robbed me in the quarrel
of the sum which I had lying by me from the price of
the vegetables I had sold, namely 16 drachmas. And on
the fifth of the same month there came this woman's husband Ammonius, also called Phimon, into my house as
if seeking my husband. Seizing my lamp, he went up into
my house, and stole and carried off a pair of bracelets of
unstamped silver of the weight of forty drachmas, my
husband being at the time away from home. I beg therefore that you will cause the accused to be brought before
you for fitting punishment. May good fortune attend
you.

Tarmuthis about 30 years old, a mark on the right
foot.

The 17th year of the Emperor Caesar Nerva Trojanus
Augustus Germanicus Dacicus. Pharmouthi 6.

We conclude that the assaulters were no respecters
of persons, because a petition [21] to the epistates of
Tebtunis voices an appeal for the apprehension of a
certain Patunis who had made an attack upon the
mother of Taarmiusis and "gave her numerous blows
upon various parts of the body, and her life is en-
dangered." Other petitions are vocal with like complaints of burglary and robbery, with violence, for
which the petitioners are insistently demanding re-
dress. We cannot resist transcribing this one: [22]

To E. . . . from Soterichus son of . . . .ion son of
Theon, of the village of Tebtunis. Some persons made a
thievish incursion into my house in the village on the
night before the 22nd of the present month Athur, taking advantage of my absence on account of my mourning
for my daughter's husband, and extracting the nails from
the doors carried off all that I had in the house, a list of
which I will furnish on the stated occasion. I accordingly
present this petition and beg that due inquiry should be
made of the proper persons, that so I may receive your
succor. The 17th year Aurelius Antoninus Caesar the
Lord, Athur 22.

Husbands must have even robbed their wives, for
there is a complaint [23] to this effect addressed by the
defrauded wife to the centurion. When Jesus likened
his coming to that of a thief (Matt. 24:43) in the
night, and described the Jericho traveler who fell
among thieves (Luke 10:30), his words must have
been enhanced in meaning by actual experiences.
Other petitions are rife with appeals for the collection of loans of money, extension of time in the payment of a note, adjustment of a difference over
weight and measure. One of these includes the words
of an anxious girl who is giving notice [24] to the centurion of the inexplicable disappearance of her father
and brother while on a hunting expedition. Here are
her exact words: "I therefore suspect that they have
met with some accident, and I present this statement,
making this matter known to you, in order that if

they have met with any accident the persons found guilty may be held accountable to me."

Wills were executed according to the conventions of legal procedure. In most cases they are written on the vertical fibers of the papyrus and, consequently, the lines are of unusual length. They detail the bequeathing of property to a husband, wife, children, or other relatives. One [25] of these very interesting wills gives the following specifications:

But if I die with this will unchanged, I set free under sanction of Zeus, Earth and Sun, for their good will and affection toward me, my slaves. . . .

I bequeath to my wife and cousin Aristous also called Apollonarion, daughter of Alexandrus, being well-disposed and showing entire faithfulness towards me, all that I may leave in the way of furniture, effects, objects of gold, clothing, ornaments, wheat, pulse, produce, and all my household stock, and my debts recorded and unrecorded.

My said wife Aristous also called Apollonarion shall pay all debts that may be proved against me; and my wife, and after her death my son Duis, shall give to my slaves and freedmen for a feast which they shall celebrate at my tomb on my birthday every year 100 drachmae of silver to be spent.

Wills were at times revoked. A will [26] made thirty years previously and deposited in the archives was rebuked by Ptolema according to a letter of the official in charge.

We cannot close this discussion without allowing

space for the bare mention of certain miscellaneous matters not exactly comprehended under the foregoing topics. For example, leases [27] of land are frequent in which specifications relative to the rent required and the method of its use are defined. Declarations [28] were also formally made guaranteeing attendance at court. One of these reveals the giving of bail for a man arrested because of debt.[29]

The minutiae of the judicial transactions set forth in this chapter introduce a legal machinery comprehensive enough to guarantee security of life, property and justice in the adjudication of the complex problems of common life. The facts outlined here are inseparably linked with the New Testament, as the quotations given under the head of pertinent references at the beginning of the chapter incontrovertibly prove.

CHAPTER VIII

THE TRADES AND PROFESSIONS

Pertinent Passages of Scripture

Is not this the carpenter, the son of Mary, and brother of James, and Joses, and Judas, and Simon?—MARK 6:3.

And his garments became glistering, exceeding white, so as no fuller on earth can whiten them.—MARK 9:3.

They that are whole have no need of a physician, but they that are sick.—MATTHEW 9:12.

And had suffered many things of many physicians, and had spent all that she had, and was nothing bettered, but rather grew worse.—MARK 5:26.

And he said unto them, Doubtless ye will say unto me this parable, Physician, heal thyself.—LUKE 4:23.

Luke, the beloved physician.—COLOSSIANS 4:14.

And because he was of the same trade, he abode with them, and they wrought; for by their trade they were tentmakers.—ACTS 18:3.

THE PERIOD embraced in our survey was by no means lifeless or unproductive. There was zestful activity along many lines which attained fruition in achievements of a highly constructive character. To get the proper perspective of this ramified activity, stimulated by a sudden liberated energy and new dynamic, it is necessary to give account of the various trades and professions which gave it expression.

It appears that the trades were supplied with workmen of approved skill who had prepared themselves by serving as apprentices. A number of "Contracts of Apprenticeship" are at hand which bear witness to this fact. We record below an agreement [1] by which Tryphon, son of Dionysius, apprenticed his son Thoonis to a weaver named Ptolemaeus for the term of one year. Weaving was the trade of Tryphon's family and he therefore desired his son to follow the same occupation.

Agreement between Tryphon, son of Dionysius, son of Tryphon, his mother being Thamounis, daughter of Onnophris, and Ptolemaeus, weaver, son of Pausirion, son of Ptolemaeus, his mother being Ophelous, daughter of Theon, both parties being inhabitants of the city of Oxyrhynchus. Tryphon agrees that he has apprenticed to Ptolemaeus his son Thoonis, whose mother is Saraeus, daughter of Apion, and who is not yet of age, for a term of one year from this day, to serve and perform all the orders given him by Ptolemaeus in respect of his weaver's art in all its branches of which Ptolemaeus has knowledge. The boy is to be fed and clothed during the whole period by his father Tryphon, who is also to be responsible for all the taxes upon him, on condition of a monthly payment to himself by Ptolemaeus of 5 drachmae on account of victuals, and at the termination of the whole period of a payment of 12 drachmae on account of clothing. Tryphon is not to have the power of taking away his son from Ptolemaeus until the completion of the period; and if there are any days on which the boy fails to attend, Tryphon shall produce him for an equivalent number of days after the period is over, or shall forfeit for each day 1 drachma of silver. The penalty for taking him away within the period shall be 100 drachmae, and an equal sum to the treasury. If Ptolemaeus fails to instruct the boy thoroughly he is to be liable to the same penalties. This contract of the apprenticeship is valid. Date and signature of Ptolemaeus.

Another typical contract [2] presents an agreement by which a boy named Pasion was apprenticed by his two brothers for one year to the weaver Pasonis in return for a loan from Jasonis of sixteen drachmae, free of interest, to be repaid at the end of the year. In still another [3] a mother apprenticed her son to a weaver for two years.

When a workman, after passing the novitiate stage, was ready to practice a trade, it seems to have been necessary for him to make due announcement of his intention. This formality was very likely made obligatory to facilitate the assessment of the regular tax imposed on trades. We give herewith an announcement [4] of this kind:

To Diogenes also called Hermaeus, ex-exegetes, scribe of the city, from Dioscorus, freedman of Sarapion, son of Sarapion son of Dio . . . , inhabitant of Oxyrhynchus in the quarter of Hermaeus. I wish to begin from the present thirteenth year of Hadrianus Caesar the lord to practice the trade of a river-worker; accordingly I present this application as above. Date.

Organized labor was well known. Almost every trade had its guild or union. It is said that there were eighty different trade unions in Rome alone. From Thyatira we hear of the organization of the tanners (who were also sometimes cobblers), leather workers, slave dealers, etc. From Italy and Egypt about a hundred different occupations have been found connected with these secret societies, among which we can reckon the guild of the shepherds, the highest of which was called the "chief shepherd." (Cf. Heb. 13:20; 1 Peter 5:4.) Each trade union was under some particular patron deity, Bacchus being naturally favored by the innkeepers, and Hercules quite as naturally by the cabmen. There were certainly doctors' unions, but probably no lawyers' unions, the lawyer giving his services gratuitously in the first century. These societies made no provision for the widow or orphans, neither did they have a sick benefit connected with them, nor did they ever make the useless attempt to get an increase in wages, so far as we know. They were influential mainly as social organizations. They first originated as "burial clubs," but soon grew into more complex trade organizations. The only way even a hard-working laborer could be sure of a decent burial in the first century was by joining one of these clubs. They were common among both Jews and heathen, and the first legal organizations were probably formed under this guise. These unions were authorized by law 22 B.C., after which they spread rapidly during the first and second centuries of our era, and with these all that was best in the life of the common people was bound up. The entrance fee, so far as can be learned, was about four or five dollars, and besides this there were monthly assessments. These clubs provided not only for a decent burial, but also gave a new impulse to life to their members, who here could breathe as nowhere else the atmosphere of freedom and self-respect. When an extra fee was paid, a memorial feast was held by the club on the anniversary of the brother's death.[5] We can get an estimate of the formidable character of these companies organized because of community of interest through the imperial suspicion and opposition which they incurred. Emperor Trajan [6] refused to approve an organization of firemen in Nocomedia on the grounds of its possible danger to the state.

The activities peculiar to these guilds are certified by their official declarations and recorded payments. Part of a series of such declarations addressed by different guilds of workmen to the logistes has been preserved. They adhere to the same formula throughout and are from the coppersmiths, beer sellers, bakers, oil sellers, and beekeepers. We give below a transcript of a declaration [7] from the coppersmiths:

To Flavius Eusebius, logistes of the Oxyrhynchite nome, from the guild of Coppersmiths of Oxyrhynchus through me Aurelius Thonius, son of Macer. We declare that at our own assessment the value given below of the goods we have in stock is that for the present month, and we swear the divine oath that our statement is correct. The value is as follows, of malleable bronze six pounds . . ., worth 1000 denarii, and of cast bronze four pounds. . . . In the consulship of Flavius Ursus and Flavius Polemius the most illustrious, Athyr 30. [Signed] I, Aurelius Thonius, make the aforesaid declaration.

A receipt [8] from the guild of iron and copper workers acknowledges a payment of six talents of silver, the price of a hundred pounds of wrought iron. The iron must have been used for public works since the payment was made from the official bank of the state revenues at Oxyrhynchus.

The great variety of trades represented by the different guilds can be ascertained through their contracts. One of these gives the agreement of some stonemasons [9] to transport 200 blocks of stone to a cistern on the estate of Flavius Apion. Some ancient stone quarries are still worked at a short distance to the north of Oxyrhynchus. Other similar contracts introduce a farm steward,[10] a horse trainer,[11] who has undertaken the superintendency of a racing stable, and some stonecutters [12] who contract to supply the stone required for building a house at Oxyrhynchus at different prices, according to the size and nature of the stones. A lead worker also gave a receipt [13] for lead and tin used in repairing the pipes of a bath. We cite below a short letter [14] in which a fuller is mentioned:

Hatres to Heras his brother, greeting. In accordance with your instructions concerning Serenus the fuller who is working with Phileas, if you have need of him send a servant for him today, the 19th. Do not neglect this, as I am keeping him. I pray for your health and prosperity. [Addressed] Deliver to Heras.

The following report of two mummifiers [15] enables us to identify another trade:

To Phacion, strategus, from Thonis son of Florus and Ptolema, aged about 35 years, having a scar upon his left wrist, and from Thonis son of Petaus and Taones, aged about 62, with no distinguishing mark, both of Oxyrhynchus, mummifiers. Today we were commissioned by you through your assistant Heraclius to inspect the dead body of Apis son of Pausis, of the said city, and to report the circumstances of the case. We therefore inspected the said body at his house. . . .

The seamy side of labor conditions is reflected in a few documents. A fragment [16] from a series of official letters concerned with a strike of slaves in a stone quarry proves labor unrest. For protection against dishonesty, a head watchman, Aurelius Menas, and his employer Apion enter into a contract [17] in which Menas obligates himself to pay twenty-four solidi in case he is proved guilty of any theft of the agricultural plant under his charge. We find the following accusation [18] in a letter:

Two brickmakers from Tampeti were brought to Ibion, and I urge you, my true and illustrious brother, to order the overseer of Tampeti to take security of them, against their absconding again and leaving their work half done.

Conspicuous among the vocations most decidedly professional in character was the physician. Even in medicine something was done. While there was usually much magic mixed up with ancient medicine, it is suggestive that Hippocrates admitted no superstition into his practice; that he correctly made hygiene the proper basis of medicine; that he discussed the quality of the water supply; and that he set down critical records of cases of fever; e.g., typhus, puerperal, malarial, and the like. Many remains of fine surgical instruments have long been known to archeologists. The medical profession was divided into many branches, in each of which specialists were doing a good business. An oculist's seal of the first century, recently found at Este, gives the specialist's name; the seal is so cleverly constructed that four different remedies can be marked with it.[19] It is believed that a fragment now in the British Museum almost certainly represents an ancient work on dentistry.[20] As we saw in a former chapter, public physicians were regularly employed by the government and often commissioned to investigate the cause of death or wounds or an accident and give due account of their findings in definitely formulated reports.[21] As is to be expected, we find the drug business in close association with the practice of medicine. The following letter [22] convinces us of the care exercised to guarantee the good quality of drugs:

Procleius to his dearest Pecysis, greeting. Be so good as to sell at your own risk good quality of those drugs of which my friend Sotas says he has need, so that he may bring them down for me to Alexandria. For if you do otherwise and give him stale stuff, which will not pass muster in Alexandria, understand that you will have to settle with me with regard to the expenses. Greet all your family. Farewell.

The medical fragments and prescriptions which have survived to our time outline myriads of remedial concoctions for the relief of the sufferers. Directions are given on the treatment of thirst in a fragment of a treatise [23] on medicine, which we give as follows:

If during the paroxysms the patient is also attacked by severe and unbearable thirst, not because of the malignity or complication of the diseases but owing to some peculiarity of the affection, this must of necessity be taken as a mischance and relieved even if such a treatment is not required by the stage of the illness. Such will be the case if the increase of the thirst is out of proportion to the height of the fever. The constitution of the patient must also be taken into consideration; for if he has general endurance but is nevertheless unable to bear the thirst. . . .

The following [24] is the translation of a column filled with a classified series of specifics for earache:

Another:—Heat an equal quantity of beaver-musk and poppy juice upon a potsherd, if possible one of Attic make, but failing that of . . .; soften by diluting with raisin wine, warm and drop in.

Another:—Dilute some gum with balsam of lilies, and add honey and rose extract. Twist some wool with oil in it round a probe, warm and drop in.

Another:—Pound some closed calices of pomegranates, drop on saffron-water, and when it becomes discoloured draw the liquor off. When required dilute as much as the bulk of a pea with raisin wine, warm, and drop in.

Stoppings for the ear against earache: Pound some Egyptian alum and insert into the ear an amount equal to the size of a pea.

Another:—Anoint a persea leaf and insert.

Another:—Thoroughly moisten a flack of wool with the gall of an ox, roll up and insert.

Another:—Pound myrrh and alum in equal quantities and insert.

Clysters for the ear against earache:

Dilute frankincense with very sweet wine and syringe the ear or use for this purpose the injections described above.

Another:—Rinse with warm onion juice.

Another:—Syringe with gall of a bull or goat or sheep, or other similar kind of gall warmed.

Another:—The sap of a pine tree, warmed to be used in the same way.

The next medical recipes [25] are given because of their strange combination with certain theological excerpts, inserted perhaps as a kind of charm:

Ingredients of a purging draught: cummin 4 drachmae, fennel 2 dr., parsley 4 dr., costus., 4 dr., mastich 4 dr., coriander 7 dr., 21 laurel berries, met. dr., ham (?). dr., penny-royal. dr., silphium (?). dr. salt . . ., vinegar. . . . men met us in the desert and said to the Lord, "Jesus, what cure is possible for the sick?" And He saith to them, "I gave olive-oil and poured forth myrrh to them that believe in the name of the Father, the Holy Spirit, and the Son."

The angels of the Lord went up to mid-heaven, suffering in their eyes and holding a spunge. The Lord saith to them, "Why came ye up, ye holy and all-pure?" (They say) "We came up to receive a remedy, Jehovah Sabaoth, for thou art mighty and strong."

For strangury, to heal the sufferer: Take the dry seed of basil thyme, crumble it with wine of Ascalon, then drink it hot.

For treating wounds: Take the fruit of a cypress, boil it and apply.[26]

There is no trace of the trained nurse as such, but we possess evidence of professional nurses in a receipt [27] for 400 drachmae for services rendered by Sarapias as nurse to the infant daughter of Tanenteris during a period of two years.

There were many other fields of professional activity manifest in the period before us. The early Christian centuries were creative. The whole civilized earth throbbed with a sudden liberated energy. It seemed as if a new intellectual dynamic had been injected into the blood of the race. Pioneers of science like Strabo were inventing geological theories which strangely resemble those of modern times; scholars like Tacitus and Livy were writing histories of such elegance and philosophic insight that they are yet classics of their kind; educators like Quintillian were originating methods of pedagogy which are only now in the twentieth century being carried into effect.

The astronomers in Alexandria were calculating eclipses, determining the equinoctial points, solstices, etc., much as is done today, and were reaching decisions concerning the size of the earth and the moon and the distance of the earth from the sun which were not far removed from those obtained by modern scholars. The sphericity of the earth was taught and illustrated in the schools, as we know from a fresco on which a terrestrial globe is represented, recently found in Rome. Nero had a pipe organ worked by machinery, a circular dining room which revolved like an astronomical dome with the sun, and a bronze hydraulic engine—found only recently in the ruins of his palace; and Boni has discovered an elevator 120 feet high connected with the emperor's palace.

The inventions of the mechanical engineers of that era have been famous ever since, and it is plain that they had been struggling somewhat successfully to master the problems connected with the power of sunlight and of confined steam which have been solved only within the last century. Hero of Alexandria is said to have constructed during the Apostolic Age the first hydraulic engine and the earliest penny in the slot machine. The gage of our modern railroad tracks is almost in exact conformity to the wheel tracks of the Roman chariot, while the director of public roads in the United States has lately declared that if modern roadbuilders were to reproduce a highway like the Appian Way, it would cost over $50,000 a mile.[28] Besides all this we find music a common accomplishment of the first century, and teaching, though despised by the Romans as a profession, occasionally entered into by a Roman knight. There were twenty grammar schools at Rome when Paul visited the city, and for over a hundred years girls as well as boys had been allowed the privileges of the schools. In many lands women had become fascinated with Greek studies, and occasionally they were employed as professors in the grammar schools. Petrie, in 1889, found at Hamara, under the head of a learned woman, a fine copy of the second book of Homer's Illiad, thumb-marked by careful study and with various critical readings marked in the margin.

CHAPTER IX

RELIGIOUS AND MORAL CONDITIONS

Pertinent Passages of Scripture

And it came to pass, as we were going to the place of prayer, that a certain maid having a spirit of divination met us, who brought her masters much gain by soothsaying.—ACTS 16:16.

And they gave heed to him, because that of long time he had amazed them with his sorceries.—ACTS 8:11.

But there was a certain man, Simon, by name, who beforetime in the city used sorcery, and amazed the people of Samaria, giving out that himself was some great one.—ACTS 8:9.

And when they had gone through the whole island unto Paphos, they found a certain sorcerer, a false prophet, a Jew, whose name was Bar-Jesus.—ACTS 13:6.

But certain also of the strolling Jews, exorcists, took upon them to name over them that had the evil spirits the name of the Lord Jesus, saying, I adjure you by Jesus whom Paul preacheth. And there were seven sons of one Sceva, a Jew, a chief priest, who did this.—ACTS 19:13-14.

But the unclean spirit, when he is gone out of the

man, passeth through waterless places, seeking rest, and findeth it not.—MATTHEW 12:43.

And he gave them leave. And the unclean spirits came out, and entered into the swine; and the herd rushed down the steep into the sea, in number about two thousand; and they were drowned in the sea.—MARK 5:13.

And he healed many that were sick with divers diseases, and cast out many demons; and he suffered not the demons to speak, because they knew him.—MARK 1:34.

And when even was come, they brought unto him many possessed with demons: and he cast out the spirits with a word, and healed all that were sick.—MATTHEW 8:16.

And when the multitude saw what Paul had done, they lifted up their voice, saying in the speech of Lycaonia, The gods are come down to us in the likeness of men.— ACTS 14:11.

And the priest of Jupiter whose temple was before the city, brought oxen and garlands unto the gates, and would have done sacrifice with the multitudes.—ACTS 14:13.

And not a few of them that practised magical arts brought their books together and burned them in the sight of all; and they counted the price of them, and found it fifty thousand pieces of silver.—ACTS 19:19.

And ye see and hear, that not alone at Ephesus, but almost throughout all Asia, this Paul hath persuaded and turned away much people, saying that they are no gods, that are made with hands.—ACTS 19:26.

And when the townclerk had quieted the multitude, he saith, Ye men of Ephesus, what man is there who knoweth not that the city of the Ephesians is temple-keeper of the great Diana, and of the image which fell down from Jupiter?—ACTS 19:35.

Idolatry, sorcery, . . .—GALATIANS 5:20.

What say I then? that a thing sacrificed to idols is anything, or that an idol is anything?—1 CORINTHIANS 10:19.

Professing themselves to be wise, they became fools, and changed the glory of the incorruptible God for the likeness of an image of corruptible man, and of birds, and four-footed beasts, and creeping things.—ROMANS 1:22-23.

For this cause God gave them up unto vile passions: for their women changed the natural use into that which is against nature: and likewise also the men, leaving the natural use of the woman, burned in their lust one toward another, men with men working unseemliness, and receiving in themselves that recompense of their error which was due.—ROMANS 1:26-27.

And after three months we set sail in a ship of Alexandria which had wintered in the island, whose sign was The Twin Brothers [Dioscuri—Castor and Pollux].—ACTS 28:11.

And in praying use not vain repetitions, as the Gentiles do: for they think that they shall be heard for their much speaking.—MATTHEW 6:7.

RELIGION is universal to man. Every tribe of men has some form of religion. The bushmen of central Australia and the Indians of Patagonia are said to represent the lowest forms of existent human life, and yet they cherish some belief in the spirit world and engage in some kind of worship. Religion has been one of the most powerful factors in human history. It is the chief differentiating characteristic of man. Although certain animals surpass men in such abilities as keenness of sense-perception and economic productiveness, no animal has ever been known to display any evidences of religious life.

The era of the New Testament is an intensely religious one.

Every people, tribe and city had its religion, but there was little moral tonic in any of them. Moral and religious ideas were in utter confusion and the hope of immortality was exceedingly vague and the future unattractive. There were lords many and gods many, male and female divinities, great gods of the nation and little gods for the household and the common affairs of daily life. The worshipers erected magnificent temples, chiseled beautiful and impressive images, supported numerous priesthoods, observed with painful care the ornate ritual and impressive ceremonies of public worship, pried into the future through divination and soothsaying, offered multitudes of sacrifices to appease the gods whose help they implored in all the affairs of life, both public and private. Religion entered into every detail of life; but the gods were themselves believed to be immoral and religion made slight demands upon the ethical sense of the people. There was little social worship or religious instruction except by a few wandering philosophers, no sacred books as among the Jews and other Oriental peoples, no inculcation of the lessons of love and right living with which we are so familiar in Christianity. The gods were feared rather than loved; the world was thought to be full of demons. The Jews of course held aloof from all this pagan religion and in general lived on a higher moral plane than their heathen neighbors whom they usually heartily despised.[1]

The papyri reward the most enthusiastic anticipations with a very satisfying array of facts potent enough to make possible the reconstruction of the kaleidoscopic ceremonials comprehended in the general term religion.

If our approach is to be logical, we must examine in the very beginning the facts relating to the priests who had the direction of the religious ritual in their charge. Great care was exercised to determine the priestly pedigree of young applicants. There were several well-marked stages required in the procedure introductory to the securing of admission to the priestly order. The following is an outline of their sequence: [2] (1) Application to the strategus or other responsible persons; (2) inquiry directed by the strategus to the local priestly college concerning the fitness of the candidate; (3) reply to the priestly college; (4) letter addressed to the high priest of Egypt and given by the strategus to the applicant, stating the facts of the case and that the necessary conditions had been fulfilled; (5) examination before the high priest, at which the candidate was produced and the letter of the strategus was read. When the candidate for the priestly order satisfactorily met these tests, he was required to submit to the rite [3] of circumcision. As a further safeguard to the priesthood, lists [4] of priests under age were kept. These were deemed necessary since the ranks of priests were regularly recruited from the younger members of their families. Affidavits [5] of priestly rank were also given. The priesthood was a hereditary office in the Greco-Roman period as in earlier times.

Certain priestly offices, particularly the superior posts in the temples, were purchased from the government. It seems that the temple at Tebtunis was administered by a board of at least ten πρεσβύτεροι whose chief members were two στολισταὶ χρόνου and a πτερόφος. But later, the chief dignitary in the temple was the προφήτης, who held a position of considerable emolument. This office had to be purchased from the government. There are many interesting details on the rivalry of successive aspirants and the nature of this office. From one [6] of these applications for purchase we cite the following:

I wish to purchase the office of prophet in the aforesaid temple which has been for a long time offered for sale, on the condition that I shall . . . and carry the palm branches and perform all the other functions attaching to the office and receive in accordance with the orders the fifth part of the whole revenue which falls to the temple, at the total price of 2200 drachmae instead of the 640 drachmae long ago offered by Marsisuchus son of Pokebkis, which sum I will, as soon as my appointment is ratified, pay into the local bank at the accustomed dates; and I and my descendants and assigns shall have the permanent ownership and possession of the office forever with all the same privileges and rights, on payment of 200 drachmae for admission.

The more subsidiary priestly offices were likewise assigned by purchase or to the highest bidder.[7] The spirit of competition became so keen among the several aspirants in their bidding, especially for the office of prophet, that judicial proceedings [8] were necessary to effect anything like an orderly settlement.

The responsibilities and activities of the priests were widely diversified, evidently demanding thorough organization and pronounced business acumen. The leading priests in each temple were compelled to send in annually to the strategus or basilico-grammateus of the nome a list of the priests and an account of the corporate receipts and expenditures for taxes or religious purposes. This return is called a γραφὴ ἱερῶν καὶ χειρισμοῦ. No specimen of these has been preserved in completeness, but their general content can be determined with reasonable accuracy from the fragmentary portions which have escaped destruction. One sacerdotal list gives the names and ages of fifty priests who were exempt from taxation and had paid definite sums for their respective offices. The receipts found among these fragments mention money payments from different villages, voluntary contributions of corn, contributions for the sacred crocodiles at Tebtunis. It appears that the priests also engaged in the cultivation of land as tenants of the state, a concession which was represented as taking the place of the σύνταξις or annual subvention from the government. According to a first century papyrus,[9] the priests made a petition to the prefect when an official threatened to raise the rent on land being worked by them. Apparently they not only leased but also subleased land.[10] They even served as collectors of the tax on weaving,[11] but their exact connection with this assignment is not clear. A receipt [12] to a priest who paid the contract price for 20,000 stems of the papyrus plant has led to the belief that the priests shared in the manufacture of papyrus writing material. This industry was likely monopolized by the government, the priests being accorded the same privileged connection with it which they enjoyed in relation to other monopolies. A contract [13] between two priests at Tebtunis for a loan of 120 drachmae implies that they qualified as money lenders, at least among themselves.

Religious functionaries and institutions helped to fill the tax coffers. The only priests who were exempt from taxation were those named in the lists of the ἀπολύσιμοι. All others were subject to the poll tax [14] and the epistates tax. The latter-named tax has been explained [15] as an impost for the salary of the epi-

states of the temple. Another interpretation declares
it to be a payment for the privilege of having an
epistates. Sacrificial calves [16] afforded another object
for taxation. Wilcken [17] has explained this tax as an
impost paid by the officiating priest upon the profits
of the sacrifice, but this view has neither received
wide acceptance nor has it been deemed well
founded. The explanation preferred by others [18] con-
ceives of it both as an impost upon the person who
offered the sacrifice and a tax levied upon the priests
of one-tenth of the profits obtained by them from
calves offered for sacrifice at the temple. A certain
tax was imposed on sales for the temple. We have an
example of such a tax in a receipt [19] from the temple
of Suchus. It was a tax amounting to 10 per cent of
the total amount charged for the sale of houses or
building sites.

The government maintained a scrupulous scrutiny
of all temple accounts through its official inspectors.
A letter [20] to a priest responsible for the temple fi-
nances gives warning of the approaching visit of a
government inspector. The recipient of the letter is
given assurance by his friend, probably a superior,
in the following lines:

Do not be disturbed on this account, as I will get you
off. So if you have time write up your books and come to
me; for he is a very stern fellow. If anything detains you,
send them on to me and I will see you through, as he has
become my friend.

As implied in this citation, the priests were not always above reproach or suspicion. But this is not our only witness. In an extant "Complaint Against a Priest," [21] five presbyter priests of the Socnopaeus temple had been ordered to inquire into the conduct of a brother-priest Panephremmis, who was charged with letting his hair grow too long and with wearing woolen garments. A certain priest was accused of having stolen the official seal [22] belonging to the temple of Heracles.

But we must give some attention to the various religious exercises and rituals found in our period.

One of the first to arrest the attention is the prominence of the oracle. The practice of consulting the local oracle in times of difficulty, which seems to have been widely extended, was doubtless encouraged by the priests as a fruitful source of gain. The following specimens of the "questions to the oracles" are informing examples. In the first one [23] Sokanobkaneus, the local deity of Bacchias, is invoked; while in the latter [24] the Dioscuri are petitioned:

To Sokanobkaneus the great, great god. Answer me, shall I remain in Bacchias? Shall I meet (him?)? Answer me this.

O lords Dioscuri, is it fated for him to depart to the city? Bring this to pass and let him come to an agreement with thy brother.

This habit of awaiting the oracular decree is reflected in the personal correspondence of the period. A letter from Lysimachus to his sister gives an illuminating sentence which reads: "It has been decided for me that I should not go down till the 25th, and as Soknebtunis the mighty god wills it I will go with boldness." [25]

Another salient feature of the contemporary religious practices is the use of magic. We give herewith a formula for obtaining an omen, of a type common in magical papyri, and purporting, as often happens with Hermetic writings, to be copied from a sacred book. To give confidence in the efficacy of the spell, the claim is made that it was used by Hermes and Isis in the search for the dismembered body of Osiris: [26]

Great is the lady Isis. Copy of a sacred book found in the archives of Hermes. The method is concerned with the 29 letters used by Hermes and Isis when searching for her brother and husband Osiris. Invoke the sun and all the gods in the deep concerning those things about which you wish to receive an omen. Take 29 leaves of a male palm, and inscribe on each of the leaves the names of the gods; then after a prayer lift them up two by two, and read that which is left at the last, and you will find wherein your omen consists, and you will obtain an illuminating answer.

However, the following specimen of a magical incantation proves the most interesting to the Bible student:

A notable spell for driving out demons. Invocation to be uttered over the head (of the possessed one). Place before him branches of olive, and standing behind him say: Hail, spirit of Abraham; hail, spirit of Isaac; hail, spirit of Jacob; Jesus the Christ, the holy one, the spirit . . . drive forth the devil from this man, until this unclean demon of Satan shall flee before. I adjure thee, O demon, whoever thou art, by the God Sarbarbarbathioth, Sarbarbarbathiuth, Sarbarbarbathioneth, Sarbarbarbphai. Come forth O demon, whoever thou art, and depart from so and so at once, at once, now. Come forth, O demon, for I chain thee with adamantine chains not to be loosed, and I give you over to black chaos in utter destruction.

The most unique example [28] of magical usage which has come under our observation is a charm consisting of a magical word repeated with the successive omission of the first and last letters so as to form an inverted triangle, which reads the same along the top and down either side, or up either side across the top and down the other side. There is a slight irregularity at the apex owing to the circumstance that the word chosen has an even number of letters. Note the word:

Αβλαναθαναβλαναμαχαραμαραχαραμαραχ

The following diagram shows the arrangement of the letters. The significance of the words has not been determined.

α β λ α ν α θ α ν α β λ α ν α μ α

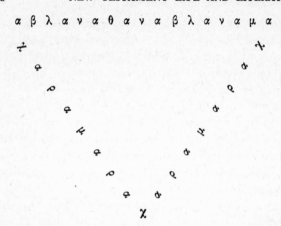

χ

A prayer for the recovery of a woman from fever follows this triangular charm.

Divination played a leading role in the religious thought of the time. We give below the translation of the one column of a Treatise on Divination [29] which has remained intact:

(If the statue of a poor man be struck by a thunderbolt and do not fall), it will be the beginning of happiness for him; but if the statue when struck by the thunderbolt falls down entirely, it indicates the destruction of his whole family. The poor man should therefore purify the statue, and sacrifice to Zeus, Wielder of Thunder, Heracles, and Fortune the Preserver in accordance with his means, and appropriate the former portent; but the portent of the fallen statue he should expiate and avert by sacrifice to the same gods. If the statues of noble men be struck by a thunderbolt. . . .

The pagan prayers are similar to the questions addressed to the oracles, discussed in a foregoing paragraph. One of these prayers [30] now before us implores the deity of some Oxyrhynchite to prevent the departure of a certain person to Alexandria. Hence travel seems to be the burden of the oracular appeals and supplications in prayer. The contrast in the prayers which are Christian in tone is very striking, but they, too, are concerned to know the divine will in making journeys.[31] The following prayer was presumably deposited in some church just as those of pagan origin were placed in the temples:

O God almighty, holy, true and merciful, Creator, Father of our Lord and Saviour Jesus Christ, reveal to me thy truth, whether it be thy will that I go to Chiout, and whether I shall find thee aiding me and gracious. So be it; Amen.

A Gnostic charm which can be listed here reveals Christian rather than pagan emphasis:

Verily guard and protect Aria from ague by day and quotidian ague and ague by night and slight fever and . . . all this thou wilt graciously do in accordance with thy will first and with her faith since she is a servant of the living God, and in order that thy name may be glorified forever.[32]

A Christian amulet [33] of the type known to have been carried by the early Christians as a counterpart to the old heathen practice, may demonstrate the difficulty of breaking completely with the established forms which Christianity was gradually supplanting.

After its introduction of the request for protection from the demon of witchcraft and pain, also all manner of disease and sickness, there follows the Lord's Prayer which is evidently substituted for the meaningless words in the old magical charms.

A most valuable survival of the Decian persecution is a collection of libelli or certificates of pagan sacrifice, which were in reality declarations which suspects were compelled to make that they had offered sacrifice to the pagan gods. They all adhere to the same stereotyped formula like the following:

> To the superintendents of offerings and sacrifices at the city from Aurelius . . . thion son Theodorus and Pantonymis, of the said city. It has ever been my custom to make sacrifices and libations to the gods, and now also. I have in your presence in accordance with the command poured libations and sacrificed and tasted the offerings together with my son Aurelius Dioscorous and my daughter Aurelia Lois. I therefore request you to certify my statement. The 1st year of the Emperor Caesar Gaius Quintus Trajanus Decius Pius Felix Augustus, Pauni 20.

Through this panorama of the pagan religions we have seen many gods and many forms, but everywhere they have proved to be utterly impotent. Their most ardent devotees are left helpless and languishing in the darkness of despair. Hence the growing dissatisfaction with multiplied charms, incantations, amulets, and powerless deities is but a natural reaction. A letter [35] of a certain Appollonius voices the state of dejection which had settled upon the contemporary mind:

I swear by Serapis—but for the fact that I am a little ashamed, you would never have seen my face—that all things are false and your gods with the rest.

There resounds through these simple records the heartache of sorrow and grief, but the religions are unable to supply sufficient solace. The following letter, which has been called the most beautiful pagan letter of consolation coming from ancient times, reveals the same sense of the inadequacy of the existent religions:

Irene to Tacunophria and Philo, good cheer! I was much grieved and wept over the blessed one, as I wept for Didymus, and everything that was fitting I did, and all who were with me. But truly there is nothing anyone can do in the face of such things. Do you therefore comfort one another. Good-bye.

Paul's words prove the adequacy of Christian consolation and bridge the distance between the dark despair of paganism and the roseate hope in Christ (1 Thess. 4:13-18). The Christian religion provides the only effective remedy for the exigencies of the present and assuring promise for the future.

But the religions of the period failed, not only because they were unable to provide a panacea capable of lifting the pall of sorrow and despair, but because they had no real moral tonic to offer. They sought to divorce religion and morals—a thing which cannot be done without the most direful consequences. We readily concede the fact, which all historians now acknowledge, that the pagan world as a whole has been painted too darkly by the earlier Christian scholars. The livid descriptions of the extremes of corruption which are found in the writings of Ovid, Petronius, Martial, Juvenal, and others pertained to the court circles and not to the middle and lower classes introduced by the papyri. Indeed, the so-called common people of every age have represented the most virile morality. Nevertheless the heathen civilization which these religions produced, at its best, compares very unfavorably with that of Christianity even at its worst. The wall paintings and public inscriptions at Pompeii, the base character of the shows most popular among all classes of the first century, the merciless and utterly inhumane treatment of slaves are but a few of the ripest fruits of the prevalent immorality. "The grossest sexual crimes are publicly referred to without shame in the witticisms inscribed upon the walls, in the private letters, and in the dramatic plays." [37] Child exposure was such a common thing that a large number of documents have come to us from Alexandria, dating near the birth of Christ, all of which prove to be contracts with women who acted as nurses for these little babies picked off the rubbish heap to be kept for slaves or used for immoral purposes.

What is the basic cause for this putrid state of morals?

The religion of the masses encouraged impurities, and the most popular poetry and novels were too vile to be sent through the mails. While the papyri have little, if anything to say on the subject, it cannot be doubted from other evidence that the temples were houses of assignation, and that even the priestesses of Isis were known to be the mistresses of certain men of letters in the Augustan age; it was actually counted a sin for a husband to object to his wife taking her turn in offering her body for hire in the name of the goddess. It is true that Mithraism with its blood purification, its hope of immortality, and its belief in future punishments and rewards, centering around the miraculous birth and ascension of Mithras, may have offered a moral tonic to the devout believer; similarly the Emperor worship was doubtless a moral advance on what preceded; nevertheless the rapid growth of Christianity was undoubtedly due to its moral and religious superiority to the religions which it superseded.[38]

Into such a dark world, in the fulness of time, Jesus came as the light of God. The darkness of the world could not hold down that Light. Through his personal ministry he brought life and light to those of his day. Through his divine Word he has brought life and light to men throughout the centuries. The more we know of the customs of the people of the first century, the better we are able to understand his Word. It is at this point that the nonbiblical papyri are proving their worth with every step made in such research.

R.F.E. completed 6-9-53 at 091

REFERENCE NOTES

Introduction

1. Meecham, *Light from Ancient Letters*, p. 25
2. Deissmann, *Light from the Ancient East*, p. 266
3. Angus, *The Environment of Early Christianity*, p. 21
4. Mason, *Outlines of Missionary History*, p. 163 f.
5. Meecham, *op. cit.*, p. 25

Chapter I

1. Deissmann, *Light on the New Testament from Records of the Graeco-Roman Period*, p. 12
2. *Schaff-Herzog Encyclopaedia*, Vol. VIII, "Papyrus"
3. *Encyclopaedia Britannica*, Vol. XX, "Papyrus"
4. *Schaff-Herzog, op. cit.*
5. *Ibid.*
6. *Encyclopaedia Britannica, op. cit.*
7. *Ibid.*
8. *Ibid.*
9. Kenyon, *The Paleography of the Greek Papyri*, p. 14. Cf. also *Encyclopaedia Britannica, op. cit.*
10. *Encyclopaedia Britannica, ibid.*
11. Finegan, *Light from the Ancient Past*, p. 308
12. Pliny, *Natural History*, XIII, 11-13
13. Milligan, *Selections from the Greek Papyri*, p. xxii
14. Milligan, *ibid.* p. xxviii
15. Baikie, *Egyptian Papyri and Papyrus Hunting*, p. 274

Chapter II

1. Kenyon, *Textual Criticism of the New Testament*, p. 25 f.
2. Deissmann, *New Light on the New Testament*, p. 50
3. Cobern, *The New Archaeological Discoveries*, p. 113
4. Hobart, *Medical Language of St. Luke*

5. Robertson, *A Grammar of the Greek New Testament in the Light of Historical Research*, p. 132
6. Deissmann, *New Light on the New Testament*, p. 65
7. Robertson, *op. cit.*, p. 128 ff.
8. Milligan, *New Testament Documents*, p. 93
9. Deissmann, *Bible Studies*, p. 44
10. Milligan, *New Testament Documents*, p. 95
11. Robertson, *op. cit.*, p. 88
12. Robertson, *ibid.*, p. 84
13. Cobern, *op. cit.*, p. 119
14. Cobern, *ibid.*, p. 109 ff.
15. Milligan, *New Testament Studies*, p. 199
16. Cobern, *op. cit.*, p. 105

Chapter III

1. Robertson, *op. cit.*, p. 80
2. Ramsay, *The Bearing of Recent Discoveries on the Trustworthiness of the New Testament*, p. 180
3. Deissmann, *The Philology of the Greek Bible*, p. 136
4. Deissmann, *Bible Studies*, p. 86 ff.
5. Robertson, *op. cit.*, p. 80
6. Robertson, *ibid.*, p. 81 ff.
7. Moulton and Milligan, *The Vocabulary of the Greek Testament Illustrated from the Papyri and Other Non-Literary Sources*
8. See Table of Abbreviations for identification of the documents cited in this chapter
9. Milligan, *Selections from the Greek Papyri*
10. Deissmann, *Biblical Studies*, p. 230 f.
11. Cobern, *op. cit.*, p. 123
12. Deissmann, *Light from the Ancient East*, p. 108 ff.

Chapter IV

1. Milligan, *Selections from the Greek Papyri*, p. 1
2. A marriage contract,   P. Eleph. I,   311-10 B.C.
3. Marriage contracts:

	P. Oxy. II, No. 265,	A.D. 81-95
	P. Oxy. III, No. 496,	A.D. 127
	P. Oxy. III, No. 497,	A.D. 125
	P. Oxy. VI, No. 905,	A.D. 170
	P. Oxy. X, No. 1273,	A.D. 260
4. Agreement of marriage,	P. Oxy. II, No. 267,	A.D. 36
5. Repudiation of a betrothal,	P. Oxy. I, No. 129,	A.D. 500
6. Repayment of a dowry,	P. Oxy. II, No. 268,	A.D. 58

7. Ptolemaic marriage laws,	P. Fay., No. 22,	A.D. 75
8. *Ibid.*		
9. Notice of birth:		
	P. Fay., No. 28,	A.D. 150
	P. Oxy. VI, No. 894,	A.D. 194
10. Milligan, *Selections from the Greek Papyri*, p. 81		
11. Gr. Ostr. I.		
12. Rescript of Gordian,	P. Tebt. II, No. 285,	A.D. 239
13. Acrostics,	P. Tebt. II, No. 278,	A.D. 25
14. Schoolboy's exercise,	P. Oxy. I, No. 124,	A.D. 200
15. Letter from Hilarion,	P. Oxy. IV, No. 744,	1 B.C.
16. A boy's letter,	P. Oxy. I, No. 119,	A.D. 150
17. Notice concerning spendthrift,	P. Flor. I, No. 99,	A.D. 100
18. Letter of a prodigal son,	P. B.G.U. III, No. 846,	A.D. 100
19. Letter of remonstrance,	P. B.G.U. II, No. 346,	A.D. 75
20. Letter of anxious mother,	P. B.G.U. II, No. 380,	A.D. 200
21. Letter of soldier,	P. B.G.U. II, No. 423,	A.D. 100
22. Epicurus to a child,	Ex. Vol. Hercul. 176,	200 B.C.
23. Polycrates to his father,	P. Par. II, 11:1,	200 B.C.
24. Isias to Hephaestion,	P. Brit. Mus., 42,	168 B.C.
25. Complaint against a husband,	P. Oxy. II, No. 281,	A.D. 40
26. Petition to a centurion,	P. Tebt. II, No. 334,	A.D. 200
27. Accusation against a husband,	P. Oxy. VI, No. 903,	A.D. 300
28. Complaint against a wife,	P. Oxy. II, No. 282,	A.D. 35
29. Deed of divorce,	P. B.G.U. III, No. 975,	A.D. 45
30. Deed of divorce,	P. Oxy. II, No. 266,	A.D. 96
31. Deed of divorce,	P. Grenf. II, No. 76,	A.D. 300
32. Deed of divorce,	P. Oxy. VI, No. 906,	A.D. 150

Chapter V

1. Census returns:		
	P. Oxy. II, No. 254,	A.D. 20
	P. Oxy. II, No. 255,	A.D. 48
	P. Oxy. II, No. 256,	A.D. 35
	P. Oxy. III, No. 479,	A.D. 157
	P. Oxy. III, No. 480,	A.D. 132
2. Receipt for poll tax,	P. Fay., No. 49,	A.D. 138
3. Receipt for poll tax,	P. Tebt. II, No. 348,	A.D. 23
4. Receipt for poll tax,	P. Tebt. II, No. 306,	A.D. 162
5. Census return,	P. Brit. Mus., No. 250,	A.D. 62
6. Census return,	P. Oxy. II, No. 254,	A.D. 20

Cf. Ramsay, *The Bearing of Recent Discoveries on the Trustworthiness of the New Testament;* Ramsay, *Was Christ Born at Bethlehem?*

7. Order to return home for
   census,   P. Brit. Mus. III,
                                    No. 904,   A.D. 104
8. Ramsay, *The Bearing of Recent Discoveries on the Trustworthiness of the New Testament*, p. 258
9. Agreement concerning tax
   collecting.   P. Tebt. II, No. 391,   A.D. 99
10. Property return,   P. Tebt. II, No. 323,   A.D. 127
11. Property return,   P. Oxy. III, No. 481,   A.D. 99
12. Revenue return,   P. Tebt. II, No. 337,   A.D. 175
13. Tax collector's return,   P. Fay., No. 41,   A.D. 186
14. Taxing lists:

                                    P. Fay., No. 40,   A.D. 162
                                    P. Tebt. II, No. 345,   28 B.C.
                                    P. Hib. I, No. 112,   260 B.C.
15. Receipt for taxing list,   P. Oxy. III, No. 515,   A.D. 134
16. Notice from tax collector,   P. Fay., No. 14,   124 B.C.
17. Receipt for salary of deputy
    tax collector,   P. Fay., No. 35,   A.D. 150
18. Cobern, *op. cit.*, p. 664
19. Extortion by a tax collector,   P. Oxy. II, No. 284,   A.D. 50
20. Extortion by a tax collector,   P. Oxy. II, No. 285,   A.D. 50
21. Cobern, *op. cit.*, p. 664
22. Sale of taxes,   P. Oxy. I, No. 44,   A.D. 75
23. Delitzsch, *Jewish Artisan Life*, p. 47
24. Cobern, *op. cit.*, p. 665 f.
25. Return of priests and revenues, P. Tebt. II, No. 298,   A.D. 107
26. Receipt for tax for temple,   P. Tebt. II, No. 281,   125 B.C.
27. Taxes on sacrifices,   P. Hib. I, No. 115,   250 B.C.
28. Ostr. I,   A.D. 171
29. *Ibid.*, footnote 27
30. Tax on weaving:

                                    P. Tebt. II, No. 305,   A.D. 135
                                    P. Fay., No. 48,   A.D. 98
31. Receipt for mason's tax,   P. Fay., No. 44,   16 B.C.
32. Tax receipt,   P. Fay., No. 15,   112 B.C.
33. Physician's tax,   P. Hib. I, No. 102,   248 B.C.
    Physician's and police tax,   P. Hib. I, No. 103,   231 B.C.
34. Tax on beer,   P. Fay., No. 47,   A.D. 61
35. Tax on wine,   P. Fay., No. 63,   A.D. 240
36. Tax on oil,   P. Fay., No. 64,   A.D. 125
37. Tax on sales:

                                    P. Tebt. II, No. 280,   126 B.C.
                                    P. Fay., No. 62,   A.D. 134
38. Bath tax,   P. Fay., No. 46,   A.D. 36

39. Receipt for various taxes,	P. Hib. I, No. 104,	225 B.C.
40. Selection of boys,	P. Fay., No. 27,	A.D. 151
41. *Ibid.*		
42. Selection of boys:		
	P. Oxy. II, No. 257,	A.D. 84
	P. Oxy. II, No. 258,	A.D. 86

Chapter VI

1. Banker's receipt,	P. Fay., No. 17,	121 B.C.
2. Banker's receipt,	P. Fay., No. 18,	73 B.C.
3. Payment through bank,	P. Fay., No. 87,	A.D. 155
4. *Ibid.*		
5. Order on a bank,	P. Fay., No. 100,	A.D. 99
6. Banking account,	P. Tebt. II, No. 347,	A.D. 125
7. Banking account,	P. Hib. I, No. 113,	260 B.C.
8. Release through a bank,	P. Tebt. II, No. 398,	A.D. 142
9. Loan through a bank,	P. Tebt. II, No. 389,	A.D. 141
10. Loan of a dowry,	P. Tebt. II, No. 386,	12 B.C.
11. Deposit of public money,	P. Tebt. II, No. 387,	A.D. 73
12. Loan on a mortgage,	P. Tebt. II, No. 390,	A.D. 167
13. Repayment of security loan:		
	P. Oxy. X, No. 1282,	A.D. 83
	P. Oxy. III, No. 507,	A.D. 169
	P. Oxy. III, No. 110,	A.D. 169
	P. Oxy. I, No. 98,	A.D. 141
	P. Oxy. VI, No. 914,	A.D. 486
14. Loan of money,	P. Oxy. II, No. 269,	A.D. 57
15. Denial of money claim,	P. Oxy. I, No. 68,	A.D. 131
16. Petition for relief,	P. Oxy. I, No. 130,	A.D. 500
17. Petition to public lawyer,	P. Oxy. VI, No. 902,	A.D. 465
18. Loan of grain and money,	P. Tebt. II, No. 388,	A.D. 98
19. Loan of corn,	P. Oxy. VI, No. 988,	A.D. 224
20. Sale of a crop,	P. Tebt. II, No. 379,	A.D. 128
21. Sale of a donkey,	P. Fay., No. 92,	A.D. 126
22. Sale of wheat,	P. Hib. I, No. 84,	300 B.C.
23. Sale of house,	P. Oxy. I, No. 99,	A.D. 55
24. Sale of land:		
	P. Oxy. I, No. 100,	A.D. 133
	P. Oxy. X, No. 1276,	A.D. 249
25. Sale of a loom,	P. Oxy. II, No. 264,	A.D. 54
26. Sale of a trichnium,	P. Oxy. X, No. 1277,	A.D. 255
27. Order of payment:		
	P. Fay., No. 16,	50 B.C.
	P. Fay., No. 18,	50 B.C.

28. *Ibid.*, P. Fay., No. 18
29. Payment as pasture rent,   P. Fay., No. 61,   A.D. 233
30. Receipt,   P. Fay., No. 60,   A.D. 169
31. Journal of Egyptian archaeology, 1915, p. 43
32. Register of paupers,   P. Brit. Mus. III, No.
                                       911,   A.D. 149
33. Letter concerning pawn,   P. Oxy. I, No. 114,   A.D. 200
34. Letter to man in money
       difficulties,   P. B.G.U. IV, No. 1079, A.D. 41
35. Cobern, *op. cit.*, p. 673 ff.

Chapter VII

1. Order for arrest,   P. Tebt. II, No. 290,   A.D. 100
2. Order for arrest,   P. Oxy. I, No. 65,   A.D. 200
3. Search for criminals,   P. Oxy. I, No. 80,   A.D. 238
4. Report of a lawsuit,   P. Oxy. I, No. 37,   A.D. 49
5. Report of a trial,   P. Tebt. II, No. 386,   A.D. 121
6. Report of a trial,   P. Tebt. II, No. 287,   A.D. 161
7. Report of an accident,   P. Oxy. III, No. 475,   A.D. 182
8. Report of mummifiers,   P. Oxy. III, No. 476,   A.D. 125
9. Report of public physician,   P. Oxy. I, No. 51,   A.D. 173
10. Report of public physician,   P. Oxy. I, No. 52,   A.D. 325
11. Wilcken, *Ostr.* I, pp. 451-454
12. *Classical Review*, April, 1900, p. 172
13. Notice of birth,   P. Fay., No. 28,   A.D. 150
14. Notice from centurion,   P. Fay., No. 38,   A.D. 275
15. Official notice,   P. Oxy. II, No. 238,   A.D. 72
16. Notice of removal,   P. Oxy. II, No. 251,   A.D. 44
17. Milligan, *Selections from the Greek Papyri*, p. 88
18. Notice of death,   P. Fay., No. 29,   A.D. 37
19. Notice of death,   P. Oxy. II, No. 262,   A.D. 77
20. Petition regarding robbery,   P. B.G.U., No. 22,   A.D. 114
21. Petition to the epistates,   P. Tebt. II, No. 283,   60 B.C.
22. Complaint of robbery,   P. Tebt. II, No. 332,   A.D. 176
23. Petition to centurion,   P. Tebt. II, No. 334,   A.D. 200
24. Petition to centurion,   P. Tebt. II, No. 333,   A.D. 216
25. Will of Acusilaus,   P. Oxy. III, No. 494,   A.D. 156
26. Revocation of a will,   P. Oxy. I, No. 106,   A.D. 135
27. Lease of land,   P. Oxy. I, No. 103,   A.D. 316
28. Promise to be at court,   P. Oxy. II, No. 260,   A.D. 59
29. Bail for a prisoner,   P. Oxy. II, No. 259,   A.D. 23

Chapter VIII

1. Contract of apprenticeship, P. Oxy. II, No. 275, A.D. 66
2. Contract of apprenticeship, P. Tebt. II, No. 384, A.D. 10
3. Contract of apprenticeship, P. Tebt. II, No. 385, A.D. 117
4. Announcement concerning P. Oxy. I, No. 1263, A.D. 128
   trade,
5. Cobern, *op. cit.*, p. 662 f.
6. Vedder, *A Short History of the Baptists*, p. 36.
7. Declaration by a guild, P. Oxy. I, No. 85, A.D. 338
8. Payment to a guild, P. Oxy. I, No. 84, A.D. 316
9. Contract of a stonemason, P. Oxy. I, No. 134, A.D. 569
10. Contract of a farm steward, P. Oxy. I, No. 136, A.D. 583
11. Contract of a horse trainer, P. Oxy. I, No. 140, A.D. 550
12. Contract of stonecutters, P. Oxy. III, No. 498, A.D. 125
13. Receipt for lead and tin, P. Oxy. VI, No. 915, A.D. 572
14. Letter of Hatres, P. Oxy. III, No. 527, A.D. 200
15. Report of mummifiers, P. Oxy. III, No. 476, A.D. 125
16. Correspondence about a strike, P. Hib. I, No. 71, 245 B.C.
17. Promise to be honest, P. Oxy. I, No. 139, A.D. 612
18. Defaulting bricklayers, P. Oxy. I, No. 158, A.D. 500
19. Cobern, *op. cit.*, p. 637
20. Cobern, *ibid.*
21. Report of accident, P. Oxy. III, No. 475, A.D. 182
22. Sale of drugs, P. Brit. Mus. II, No.
   356, A.D. 50
23. Medical fragment, P. Tebt. II, No. 272, A.D. 175
24. Medical prescriptions, P. Oxy. II, No. 234, A.D. 200
25. Medical recipes, P. Oxy. XI, No. 1384, A.D. 400
26. Baikie, *Egyptian Papyri and Papyrus Hunting*, p. 313 f.
27. Wages for nurse, P. Oxy. I, No. 91, A.D. 187
28. Cobern, *op. cit.*, p. 635 ff.

Chapter IX

1. McGlothlin, *The Course of Christian History*, p. 6
2. Report of examination, P. Tebt. II, No. 291, A.D. 162
   Application for circumcision, P. Tebt. II, No. 292, A.D. 189
3. Report on application for
   permission to circumcise, P. Tebt. II, No. 293, A.D. 187
4. List of priests under age, P. Oxy. X, No. 1256, A.D. 282
5. Affidavit of priestly rank, P. Oxy. X, No. 1265, A.D. 336
6. Purchase of priestly office, P. Tebt. II, No. 294, A.D. 146
7. Purchase of priestly office, P. Tebt. II, No. 295, A.D. 126

8. Purchase of priestly office,	P. Tebt. II, No. 297,	A.D. 123
9. Petition of priests,	P. Tebt. II, No. 302,	A.D. 71
10. Lease of temple land,	P. Tebt. II, No. 309,	A.D. 116
11. Receipt for tax,	P. Tebt. II, No. 305,	A.D. 135
12. Receipt for papyrus,	P. Tebt. II, No. 308,	A.D. 174
13. Loan of money,	. Tebt. II, No. 312,	A.D. 123
14. Receipt for tax,	P. Tebt. II, No. 306,	A.D. 162
15. *Ibid.*		
16. Receipt for tax,	P. Tebt. II, No. 307,	A.D. 208
17. Wilcken, *op. cit.*, p. 101		
18. *Ibid.*		
19. Receipt for tax,	P. Tebt. II, No. 281,	125 B.C.
20. Temple accounts,	P. Tebt. II, No. 315,	A.D. 125
21. Complaint against priest,	P. B.G.U. I, No. 16,	A.D. 159
22. Temple seal correspondence,	P. Hib. I, No. 72,	241 B.C.
23. Question to oracle,	P. Fay., No. 137,	A.D. 50
24. Question to oracle,	P. Fay., No. 138,	A.D. 100
25. Letter of Lysimachus.	P. Tebt. II, No. 284,	50 B.C.
26. Magical formula,	P. Oxy. VI, No. 886,	A.D. 200
27. Magical incantation,	P. Par., No. 574,	A.D. 200
28. Magical charm,	P. Tebt. II, No. 275,	A.D. 200
29. Treatise on divination,	P. Oxy. VI, No. 885,	A.D. 175
30. Petition to pagan deity,	P. Oxy. VI, No. 923,	A.D. 175
31. Christian prayer,	P. Oxy. VI, No. 925,	A.D. 450
32. Gnostic charm,	P. Oxy. VI, No. 924,	A.D. 300
33. Wilcken, in *Archiv* I, p. 431 f.		
34. Certificate of sacrifice,	P. Oxy. IV, No. 658,	A.D. 250
35. Letter of despair,	P. Par., No. 47,	150 B.C.
36. Letter of consolation,	P. Oxy. I, No. 115,	A.D. 125
37. Cobern, *op. cit.*, p. 682		
38. Cobern, *ibid.*, p. 667 f.		

ABBREVIATIONS FOR PAPYRUS DOCUMENTS

B G U — Berlin Griechische Urkunden I-VIII
P Alex — Papyrus du Mussee d' Alexandrie
P Amh — The Amherst Papyri I-II
P Cairo Zen — Zenon Papyri I-III
P Cornell — Greek Papyri in the Library of Cornell University
P Eleph — Elephantine Papyri
P Fay — Fayum Towns and Their Papyri
P Flor — Papiri Fiorentini I-III
P Giss — Griechische Papyri zu Giessen I
P Goodsp — A Group of Greek Papyrus Texts, Ed. E. J. Goodspeed
Gr. Ostr — Griechische Ostraca aus Aegypten und Nubien
P Grenf — An Alexandrian Erotic Fragment
P Grenf II — New Classical Fragments
P. Hib — The Hibeh Papyri I
P Lond — Greek Papyri in the British Museum
P Oxy — The Oxyrhynchus Papyri
P Par — Paris Papyri
P Par 574 — The Paris Magical Papyrus
P Petr — The Flinders Petrie Papyri
P Ryl — Papyri in John Rylands Library
P Tebt — The Tebtunis Papyri
P Thead — Papyrus de Theadelphie
P Tor — Papyri Graeci Regii Taurinensis Musei Aegyptii

TABLE OF EGYPTIAN MONTHS

Θώθ	Aug. 29–Sept. 27
Φαῶφι	Sept. 28–Oct. 27
Ἀθύρ	Oct. 28–Nov. 26
Χοίαχ	Nov. 27–Dec. 26
Τῦβι	Dec. 27–Jan. 25
Μεχείρ	Jan. 26–Feb. 24
Φαμενώθ	Feb. 25–Mar. 26
Φαρμοῦθι	Mar. 27–Apr. 25
Παχών	Apr. 26–May 25
Παῦνι	May 26–June 24
Ἐπείφ	June 25–July 24
Μεσορή	July 25–Aug. 23
ἐπαγόμεναι ἡμέραι	Aug. 24–Aug. 28

SOURCE MATERIALS

ENCYCLOPEDIAS

The Encyclopedia Americana
New York: Encyclopedia Americana Corp., 1918
The Encyclopedia Biblica
London: Adam and Charles Black, 1899
The Encyclopaedia Britannica
Chicago: University of Chicago Press, 1946
The Catholic Encyclopedia
New York: Robert Appleton, 1907
Hastings' Dictionary of the Bible
New York: Charles Scribner's Sons, 1898
The International Standard Bible Encyclopaedia
Grand Rapids: Wm. B. Eerdmans Publishing Company, 1947
The Jewish Encyclopedia
New York: Universal Jewish Encyclopedia Corp., 1939
The New International Encyclopaedia
New York: Dodd, Mead and Company, 1908
The Encyclopedia of Religion and Ethics
New York: Charles Scribner's Sons, 1908
The New Schaff-Herzog Encyclopedia of Religious Knowledge
New York: Funk and Wagnalls Company, 1908

Papyrus Documents

(See Table of Abbreviations)

Books

Abbott, F. F. *Common People of Ancient Rome.*
New York: Charles Scribner's Sons, 1911

Angus, S. *The Environment of Early Christianity.*
New York: Charles Scribner's Sons, 1931

Baikie, James. *Egyptian Papyri and Papyrus Hunting.*
London: The Religious Tract Society, 1925

Barton, G. A. *Archaeology and the Bible.*
Philadelphia: American Sunday School Union, 1925

Beecher, W. J. *Reasonable Biblical Criticism.*
Philadelphia: The Sunday School Times Company, 1911

Bell, H. I. *Recent Discoveries of Biblical Papyri.*
Oxford: Clarendon Press, 1937

Blass, F. *Philology of the Gospels.*
New York: The Macmillan Company, 1898

Boak, A. E. R. *Papyri from Tebtunis.*
Ann Arbor: University of Michigan Press, 1933

Case, S. J. *The Evolution of Early Christianity.*
Chicago: The University of Chicago Press, 1914

Cobern, C. M. *Recent Explorations in Palestine.*
Meadville, Pennsylvania: The Collegiate Publishing Company, 1916

Cobern, C. M. *The New Archaeological Discoveries and Their Bearing Upon the New Testament.*
New York: Funk and Wagnalls Company, 1929

Cowley, A. *Aramaic Papyri of the Fifth Century.*
Oxford: Clarendon Press, 1923

Dale, R. W. *The Living Christ.*
New York: A. C. Armstrong and Son, 1890

Dana, H. E. *The New Testament World.*
Fort Worth: Pioneer Publishing Company, 1928

Davis, W. H. *Greek Papyri of the First Century.*
New York: Harper and Brothers Publishers, 1933

Deissmann, A. *Bible Studies.*
Edinburgh: T. and T. Clark, 1909

Deissmann, A. *Light from the Ancient East.*
New York: George H. Doran Company, 1910

Deissmann, A. *New Light on the New Testament from the Records of the Graeco-Roman Period.*
New York: Charles Scribner's Sons, n.d.

Deissmann, A. *The New Testament in the Light of Modern Research.*
Garden City: Doubleday, Doran and Company, Inc. 1929

Deissmann, A. *Philology of the Greek Bible.*
London: Hodder and Stoughton, 1908

Delitzsch, F. *Jewish Artisan Life.*
New York: Funk and Wagnalls Company, 1883

Edersheim, Alfred. *Sketches in Jewish Social Life.*
Boston: A. I. Bradley and Company, n.d.

Finegan, Jack. *Light from the Ancient Past.*
Princeton: Princeton University Press, 1946

Goodspeed, E. J. *Greek Papyri from the Cairo Museum.*
Chicago: University of Chicago Press, 1902

Goodspeed, E. J. and Colwell, E. C. *Greek Papyrus Reader.*
Chicago: University of Chicago Press, 1935

Grant, C. M. *Between the Testaments.*
New York: Fleming H. Revell Company, n.d.

Grant, F. C. *Economic Background of the Gospels.*
London: Oxford University Press, 1926

Gregory, C. R. *Canon and Text of the New Testament.*
    New York: Charles Scribner's Sons, 1912
Handcock, P. S. P. *The Archaeology of the Holy Land.*
    New York: The Macmillan Company, 1916
Harnack, A. *Date of Acts and the Synoptic Gospels.*
    New York: G. P. Putnam's Sons, 1911
Harnack, A. *The Sayings of Jesus.*
    New York: G. P. Putnam's Sons, 1908
Harnack, A. *Luke the Physician.*
    New York: G. P. Putnam's Sons, 1911
Hunt, A. S. and Edgar, C. C. *Select Papyri.*
    Harvard: Harvard University Press, 1934
Julicher, A. *Introduction to the New Testament.*
    London: Smith, Elder and Company, 1904
Kenyon, F. G. *Evidence of the Papyri with Regard to
    Textual Criticism of the New Testament.*
    Oxford: Oxford University Press, 1905
Kenyon, F. G. *Our Bible and the Ancient Manuscripts.*
    New York: Harper and Brothers, 1940
Kenyon, F. G. *Recent Developments in the Textual
    Criticism of the New Testament.*
    London: Oxford Press, 1933
Kenyon, F. G. *The Paleography of the Greek Papyri.*
    Oxford: University of Oxford Press, 1899
Kennedy, H. A. A. *Saint Paul and the Mystery Religions.*
    London: Hodder and Stoughton, 1913
Mason, A. D. *Outlines of Missionary History.*
    New York: George H. Doran Company, 1912
Matthews, Shailer. *The History of the New Testament
    Times in Palestine.*
    New York: The Macmillan Company, 1899
McGlothlin, W. J. *The Course of Christian History.*
    New York: The Macmillan Company, 1925

Meecham, H. G. *Light from Ancient Letters.*
New York: The Macmillan Company, 1923
Milligan, George. *Here and There Among the Papyri.*
London: Hodder and Stoughton, 1922
Milligan, George. *The New Testament Documents.*
London: Macmillan and Company, 1913
Milligan, George. *Selections from the Greek Papyri.*
Cambridge: Cambridge University Press, 1912.
Moulton, J. H. *From Egyptian Rubbish Heaps.*
London: The Epworth Press, 1927
Moulton, J. H. *Grammar of the Greek New Testament.*
Edinburgh: T. and T. Clark, 1908
Moulton, J. H. and Milligan, George. *The Vocabulary of the Greek New Testament Illustrated from the Papyri and Other Non-Literary Sources.*
London: Hodder and Stoughton, 1930
Petrie, W. M. F. *History of Egypt.*
London: Methuen Company, 1895
Petrie, W. M. F. *The Religion of Ancient Egypt.*
London: Archibald Constable and Company, 1908
Ramsay, W. M. *The Bearing of Recent Discoveries on the Trustworthiness of the New Testament.*
London: Hodder and Stoughton, 1920
Ramsay, W. M. *Was Christ Born at Bethlehem?*
London: Hodder and Stoughton, 1898
Robertson, A. T. *A Grammar of the Greek New Testament in the Light of Historical Research.*
London: Hodder and Stoughton, 1915
Robertson, A. T. *Introduction to the Textual Criticism of the New Testament.*
New York: George H. Doran Company, 1925
Tucker, T. G. *Life in the Roman World of Nero and Saint Paul.*
New York: The Macmillan Company, 1911

Vedder, H. C. *A Short History of the Baptists.*
> Philadelphia: American Baptist Publication Society, 1907

Wenter, J. G. *Life and Letters in the Papyri.*
> Ann Arbor: University of Michigan Press, 1936

Wikgren, A. *Hellenistic Greek Texts.*
> Chicago: University of Chicago Press, 1937

Wilcken, U. *Griechische Ostraca aus Aegypten und Nubien.*
> Leipzig, 1899

Wright, C. H. H. *Light from Egyptian Papyri on Jewish History Before Christ.*
> London: Williams and Norgate, 1908

JOURNALS

American Journal of Archaeology
> July, 1933; July, 1935; April, 1945

American Journal of Philology
> April, 1937; January, 1938; October, 1938; April, 1940; April, 1943; July, 1944

Classical Philology
> July, 1924; July, 1927; April, 1930; July, 1932; January, 1933; July, 1933; April, 1935; April, 1936; April, 1937; January, 1938; April, 1939; January, 1941

Classical Review
> May, 1926; February, 1932; December, 1933; December, 1934; September, 1943

Harvard Theological Review
> January, 1931; July, 1933; April, 1946

Journal of Egyptian Archaeology
> July, 1915; July, 1939

John Rylands Library Bulletin
> January, 1934; October, 1937; October, 1938